MW00903507

ISRAEL
IN THE
BIBLICAL
WORLDVIEW
AN INTRODUCTION

ISRAEL
IN THE
BIBLICAL
WORLDVIEW
AN INTRODUCTION

About the author

Copyright © 2022-2023 Perry Trotter

ISBN: 9798394757457

ABBREVIATIONS
USED IN THE FOOTNOTES

AC	*Abrahamic Covenant*
ESV	*English Standard Version*
GLP	*The Gospel and the Land of Promise*
JETS	*Journal of the Evangelical Theological Society*
LTJM	*The Life and Times of Jesus The Messiah*
LXX	*Septuagint*
MHMP	*The Moody Handbook of Messianic Prophecy*
MIOT	*The Messiah in the Old Testament*
NET	*New English Translation*
NASB	*New American Standard Bible*
NIV	*New International Version*
NT	*New Testament*
OC	*Old Covenant*
OT	*Old Testament*
RT	*Replacement Theology*
WRSM	*What the Rabbonim Say About Moshiach*

URLs in the footnotes were accessed 2022-23

Cover image © 2008 Perry Trotter
Wilderness of Zin, near Sde Boker, Israel

Thanks

Heartfelt thanks are due,
whether for helpful feedback, proofreading,
prayer, encouragement or support over the years,
or endorsement:

*David Anderson, Mottel Baleston, Paul Moon,
Paul Henebury, Graham Preston, Margaret Canter,
David Tweed, Paul Cohen, Roland van Noppen,
Charles Hlavac, Tony and Diana Wood,
Mark Musser, Alf Cengia, Robert Nicholson*

Dedication

To Sheree,
for her support, patience and love,
for walking this unpopular path with me for
decades,
for her expertise, for encouraging me to write,
and to our beloved children,
Ajhalia, Zahn, Ylia and Avya.

CONTENTS

Endorsements

Israel in the Biblical Worldview is a concise, reader-friendly yet deceptively full study of the place and importance of Israel in Scripture. Many biblical studies take a long time to get to the point, by which time the student's attention span is flagging. Happily, this study is different; its bitesize chapters deliver solid information in an accessible format and a winning style.

Trotter knows the Bible. He knows that God has a magnificent future for Israel, and he knows that Israel actually means Israel, not the Church! The book is a commendable piece of work from a sound teacher. What more could one want?

Paul Martin Henebury, PhD, MTS, MDiv
Telos Theological Ministries, USA, Author at DrReluctant

The promise of Israel's ultimate restoration is one of the Bible's most enduring motifs. In this patient and informative study, Perry Trotter thoroughly examines the bases of this promise to the Jewish people, its evolution in the Bible, and how denial of this precept has been a continuous source of antisemitism for centuries.

Paul Moon ONZM
DLitt, PhD, FLS, FRSA, FRAI, FRGS, FRHistS
Auckland, New Zealand

Israel in the Biblical Worldview is a remarkable piece of scholarship. It invites us to align our thinking about the Messiah and Israel closely with Scripture, and provokes us to a much needed conversation and re-examination of replacement theology. Antisemitism and replacement theology are not synonymous, but it is clear that the great tragedy of the Holocaust was born out of replacement theology and the irrational hatred of a people group.

I was deeply moved to read of several Christian Kaumatua (elders) of Nga Puhi who travelled to Wellington after world War II to offer 1200 acres of their land to Jewish refugees. Many of my husband's ancestors suffered indescribable cruelty in the European concentration camps, and those who survived desperately needed the help of caring people like Nga Puhi. This outstanding book by Perry Trotter addresses some of the difficult issues around the Jewish people, a people destined only to be a blessing to others.

Margaret Canter (Leighton), PhD, University of London
Tauranga, New Zealand

Trotter's case against replacement theology and antisemitism introduces the reader to the Jewishness of Jesus and the covenants. An invaluable primer to thinking biblically about the people and land of Israel.

Robert Nicholson
President and Founder, Philos Project, USA

12

Recent years have seen an explosion in misinformation about Israel and the situation in the Middle East. Online video sites and social media peddle false narratives of half-truths and outright falsehoods. Frequently these are malevolent and racist against the Jewish people. As a Jewish believer in Messiah Jesus, it is heartbreaking and concerning to me as I see some of my fellow believers taken in by these toxic falsehoods.

This book by Perry Trotter has no agenda but that of Scripture, and clearly lays out God's plan and program for the Jewish people and the nation of Israel and does that with utmost fidelity to God's Word.

God's love extends to both Jew and Arab equally, and when biblically understood we see His plan to bring atonement to all who will believe. Reading this compact book will equip you to understand the overall plan of God, and the small investment of time will be well worth your while.

Mottel Baleston, Messianic Jewish Educator
New Jersey, USA

The Messiah revealed Himself to me in my early twenties and brought me in contact with Keith and Margaret Relf, who became my Christian mentors. Their love for Jesus, commitment to the Word and to Israel, was contagious. My journey of more than fifty-five years continues to be 'salted' with the importance of God's view of Israel as foundational to our faith, our daily lives, and our future.

My very long career in education has included a passion to promote a biblical understanding of Israel and God's heart for the holy land and its people. With God's leading, Perry and Dr Sheree Trotter have become important advisers to me on these matters and some of my educational colleagues. This book is one of the fruits of their hard work and scholarship. It is my joy to commend this book for your prayerful consideration.

Graham Preston MNZM
Tauranga, New Zealand

Perry Trotter has written a valuable and concise summary of the church's sad role in misrepresenting the text of Scripture with its false notion of what is generally characterized as replacement theology.

Many Christians believe the church has replaced Israel. Since the Messianic ministry of Jesus was largely rejected the first go around by His own people, all too many have falsely concluded that the New Testament Church has superseded, nay even changed God's worldwide salvation program granted through the nation of Israel. In so doing, Christians too often misread God's foundational covenants promised to the patriarchs, allegorically reinterpret the land promise that denies its origi-

14

nal intent, and misuse Christology to rob the essential Jewish character of both the Davidic and New Covenants so they are presumed to be entirely fulfilled by the New Testament Church. Armed with such misunderstandings, Christians commonly entertain various forms of antisemitism that on the surface appear either justifiable or innocuous. It is thus unsurprising that Israel's eschatological future is also deeply mischaracterized through a very subtle form of Christianization that confiscates the strong Jewish elements deeply rooted in the Old Testament covenants and prophecies which must be fulfilled by God's predetermined plan for the ages.

If God does not keep His promises to Israel, then how does the Church know it will keep His promises to Christians? Perry Trotter does an excellent job explaining why replacement theology is fraught with many serious theological problems and grave concerns relative to a biblical understanding of God's people Israel that cannot be ignored.

Dr R Mark Musser
Author of "Nazi Ecology: The Oak Sacrifice of the Judeo-Christian Worldview in the Holocaust"

FOREWORD

David R Anderson, PhD
President, Grace School of Theology
Distinguished Professor of
Systematic Theology and Biblical Languages

I t has been said that one of the kings of Prussia asked his spiritual advisor for definitive proof that God exists. The advisor's answer was simple:
"The Jew, your Highness. The Jew."

He was referring to the very existence of ethnic Jews after centuries of scattering and miscegenation among the Gentiles. It is an anthropological anomaly. No other ethnic group has undergone a diaspora like the Jews without complete assimilation and loss of identity. But the Bible has a number of prophecies about the Jews and promises given to the Jews that beg for fulfillment if indeed the God of the Bible does exist and can be taken at His word. Thus, the very fact that the Jews as an ethnic group still exist is one of the very best proofs of God. His promises to literal, physical Israel have not been broken.

Yet God's purpose for and the existence of the Jews has been threatened from the time of their slavery in Egypt until today. These threats to their existence we call *antisemitism*. In half of this monograph Perry Trotter traces the biblical role of literal Israel and the future kingdom of God. He exposes the anti-literalism of replacement theology, the claim of most Covenant theologians that the universal Church has replaced Israel in God's theocratic program, meaning the promises originally intended by God for Israel will be fulfilled in the Church as a result of Israel's rejection of Christ as their King. Trotter traces replacement theology all the way back to Origen, and beyond. Origen was well known for his allegorization of the biblical narrative, an approach that gathered momentum with Augustine and spread throughout the Church over the centuries.

If the Church has replaced Israel in God's kingdom program, there is no longer a use for the Jewish people, or so reason many of the replacement theologians. This kind of theology was promulgated by Martin Luther whose writings to this effect were used by Adolf Hitler to justify the Holocaust. Trotter does a masterful job of following the trail of antisemitism under the veil of anti-Zionism. He even zeros in on anti-Zionism in his own native county, New Zealand. From the pogroms in Russia to the Arab-Israeli conflict, he outlines the escalation of antisemitism over the last 150 years. And he demonstrates that behind all the human attempts at genocide of the Jews is a spiritual enemy, Satan himself.

Much more needs to be said about the importance of Israel in God's prophetic program - and that is precisely what Trotter does for us in this book. His efforts are a masterful compilation of the pertinent prophecies and the antisemitic history of the past two thousand years to help us understand the reason the Jews still exist and their irreplaceable importance in God's theocratic program for mankind.

So, buckle up - you're in for a ride!

David R Anderson
March 2023

PART I

And I will put enmity between you and the woman, and between your offspring and hers;

he will crush your head, and you will crush his heel.

Genesis 3:15

1

WHO IS THE MESSIAH?

T he Bible opens with a brief account of the creation, followed immediately by the fall of man.[1] Amidst God's dreadful pronouncement of curses upon the serpent, the man and the woman, is a somewhat enigmatic promise that the woman's seed will crush the serpent's head.[2] In the process, this promised One's heel will be crushed. Thus begins the gradual unveiling of the coming redeemer and the cosmic conflict in which He will be victor.

As we read through the documents we now call the Old Testament, additional data concerning the

---

[1] Gen 1:1-3:8
[2] Gen 3:15 This prediction, along with several others cited in this chapter, is briefly addressed in *Appendix: Messianic Prophecy,* along with selected rabbinic views of the various predictions.

prophesied One is progressively revealed until a comprehensive picture of His identity and career are in view.[3]

Numerous titles are given to the coming One. From our standpoint, the most familiar is Messiah,[4] though it is only rarely used in the Old Testament.[5]

At first, it is not at all apparent that it is a singular individual who is in view, but over time the various themes and predictions converge in the One Christians believe to be the Messiah, Jesus of Nazareth. Much is to be gained from a consideration of His many offices and titles.[6]

Through Abraham, Isaac and Jacob, God establishes Israel as the instrument through which blessings to all mankind will be mediated, chief of which will be the Messiah.[7]

---

[3] The NT nowhere labels the Hebrew Scriptures "Old Testament" (2 Cor 3:14 is a reference to the Mosaic covenant.) The Hebrew Scriptures constituted the Bible of Jesus and His earliest followers. The term "New Testament" as a title for the writings of the apostles and their associates is thought to have originated with Tertullian.

[4] Or Christ. Messiah is a transliteration of the Hebrew *Mashiach*, *anointed one*. Christ comes to us from *Christos*, a Greek translation of the Hebrew *Mashiach*.

[5] Many are seen as *anointed ones* in the OT, including priests (e.g. Lev 4:3), kings (e.g. 1 Sam 26:9, Isa 45:1), patriarchs (e.g. Ps 105:15). Among a few texts that use the term of the One Christians call Messiah or Christ are Ps 2:2 and Dan 9:25.

[6] See *Appendix: Messianic Prophecy*

[7] Gen 12:1-3,7; 15:1-19; 26:2-4; 28:12-15; Rom 9:5

Late in Jacob's life it is revealed that a kingly ruler will descend from his son Judah.[8]

Via Balaam, whom Balak hoped would curse Israel, we learn that the coming King will one day slaughter Israel's enemies.[9] A curse is promised upon those that curse Israel, but blessing for blessing, just as had been revealed to Abraham centuries prior.[10]

Moses speaks of a future prophet like himself, One in whose mouth God will put His own words, and to whom the Israelites will be accountable.[11]

Of all the prophets, Isaiah had most to say about the coming Messiah. The substitutionary atoning death of Messiah is revealed within lengthy passages concerning the servant of the Lord, all written seven hundred years prior to His first coming.[12] A deeply unsettling picture is painted: although ultimately He will be supremely exalted,[13] He will be appallingly disfigured, despised, rejected, and a man of sorrows with nothing to attract Isaiah's people.[14] Though innocent He will bear the sins of many, and be pierced and

---

[8] Gen 49:10

[9] Num 22:11; 23:7,11; 24:7,8,17-19

[10] Num 24:9; Gen 12:3 At that time, *Abram*.

[11] Deut 18:15-19 (Note the expectation recorded in Jn 1:21; 6:14).

[12] Isa 53:4-12

[13] Isa 52:13 (compare similar phrase in Isa 6:1)

[14] Isa 53:2,3,14

crushed for iniquities not His own.[15] Both His death and resurrection are explicitly revealed.[16] Isaiah sees His humiliation and compassion[17] and that redemption will be extended to non-Jews.[18]

The same prophet describes Messiah as a divine King, yet a child in the lineage of David.[19] Isaiah offers a beautiful portrayal of the gentleness of the coming One, saying *a bruised reed He will not break* and that He will bind up the brokenhearted.[20] Yet somehow He will also be a blood drenched warrior, One to execute vengeance.[21]

Other prophets reveal He will reign from Jerusalem with a rod of iron,[22] having regathered His dispersed Jewish brethren from around the world.[23]

The Old Testament text most frequently quoted by New Testament writers reveals Messiah as One who will sit for a time at the right hand of God,[24]

---

[15] Isa 53:5,6,9,11,12

[16] Isa 53:9-12

[17] Isa 42:3; 49:7; 50:6

[18] Isa 49:6; 52:15

[19] Isa 9:6,7 Three of several titles in v6 could only refer to the divine, implying He will be the God-man.

[20] Isa 42:3; 61:1

[21] Isa 34:2-8; 35:4; 61:2; 63:1-6

[22] Jer 23:5,6; Zech 14:4-9; Ps 2:6,9 (Rev 12:5)

[23] Jer 23:3-9; 16:14,15; 31:8-10; Deut 30:3; Zeph 3:14-20; Ezek 36:24

[24] Ps 110:1 (Ps 110 is quoted in Matt, Mark, Luke, Acts, Heb).

will be a priest, and will ultimately judge the nations, heaping up the dead.[25]

Daniel provides a remarkable timeline, revealing Messiah must come - and die - before the destruction of the second temple (at that time unbuilt).[26]

Many prophets contribute to a detailed portrait of Messiah till He is seen to be a Prophet, Priest, King and more. Strikingly, the volume of Old Testament passages that, with the benefit of hindsight, relate to His second coming, outweigh those relating to His first.

When we reach the New Testament we find great expectation among faithful Israelites, and even a number of Babylonian Magi.[27] John the Baptist declares Messiah to be the Lamb of God, a concept anchored in the Hebrew Scriptures.[28] Jesus precisely fulfills many prophecies, but, importantly, many still remain unfulfilled. In a post-resurrection appearance Messiah assures His disciples that those predictions too, must be fulfilled.[29]

The New Testament of course provides much additional data on Messiah's return. The nature of

---

[25] Ps 110:4-6

[26] Dan 9:24-27 https://www.messiah.com.es/daniel-9

[27] Matt 2:1,2; Luk 2:25-32; 36-38; Jn 1:41-45

[28] Jn 1:29,36; Gen 22:8; Isa 53:7

[29] Luke 24:44 (see also Rom 15:8)

non-Jewish blessing and inclusion is elucidated and the church is established.[30]

The believer's challenge is to embrace and affirm all that is revealed concerning the Messiah, including those neglected aspects of His career as yet unfulfilled.[31] In doing so one gains clarity and wisdom for this age. One's worship and reverence for the *seed of the woman* should be grounded in all that He has revealed Himself to be.

---

[30] Acts 2; Rom 11:11-24; 1 Cor 12:13; Eph 2,3

[31] Those OT messianic *predictions* that were fulfilled at Jesus' first coming, were fulfilled *as written*. It is important to recognise that the remaining predictions will be fulfilled in like manner. (Note the distinction between direct OT messianic prediction versus mere mention of, or allusion to, an OT text by the NT. The NT quotes the OT in multiple ways, only a minority of which constitute fulfillment of a direct OT prediction, in which the details of an OT predicted event or person directly correspond to the details of the NT event or person.) Many theologians instead insist that *all* messianic predictions were fulfilled at Messiah's first coming. This does violence to the plain meaning of the texts and has significant implications for the integrity and coherence of the biblical message. See Chapter 5, *Replacement Theology* and *Appendix: Messianic Prophecy.*

*I will make you
into a great nation
and I will bless you;*

*I will make
your name great,
and you will be a blessing.*

Genesis 12:2

2

WHO IS ISRAEL?

The definition of a Jew or Israelite in Scripture is essentially quite simple: a descendant of Abraham, Isaac and Jacob.[32] But first, let's ask the question: *Why does it matter?*

Among several reasons are the following:

- Throughout history there have been incessant and determined efforts to obfuscate,[33] deny[34]

---

[32] *Jew* and *Israelite* (and their respective variants) are used interchangeably from the later biblical period e.g. Acts 2:14, 22. Among referents of the term Israel: the patriarch, the nation, the remnant, the land.

[33] Replacement theologians have been among the chief offenders. Attempts to "redefine" and "reinterpret" biblically established definitions usually appeal to several NT proof texts, quoted out of context. See Part II

[34] e.g. The debunked Khazar theory.
https://forward.com/opinion/382967/ashkenazi-jews-are-not-khazars-heres-the-proof/
https://pubmed.ncbi.nlm.nih.gov/25079123/

or expropriate Jewish identity[35] (and of course there have been attempts to annihilate the Jews as a people).[36] Arguably, this hostility is inexplicable apart from a recognition of the spiritual battlefield and the central role occupied by the Jews.[37]

- The ongoing existence and distinction of the Jewish people are essential to numerous biblical themes and future events, including Messiah's return to the earth.[38]

- Put another way: the coherence of the biblical account requires the permanence of the Jewish people. A simple example: *Hear the word of the LORD, O nations; proclaim it in distant coastlands: 'He who scattered Israel will gather them and will watch over his flock like a shepherd.'*[39]

---

[35] e.g. Jehovah's Witnesses, British Israelism, some expressions of replacement theology. See Part II.

[36] e.g. the Khelmnitsy massacres 1648-49, the Holocaust, and the war against the modern Jewish state 1948 to present.
More generally, the non-Jewish world's preoccupation with the Jews is remarkable. e.g. *And in the vast archives of material that survive from Early Modern and Modern Europe and its cultural colonies, it is easy enough to demonstrate that words like Jew, Hebrew, Semite, Israelite, and Israel appear with a frequency stunningly disproportionate to any populations of living Jews in those societies.* David Nirenberg, *Anti-Judaism*, p7.

[37] See Chapter 9, *Antisemitism and Its Unseen Cause*

[38] e.g. the regathering of Israel (Deut 4:27-31), the messianic kingdom (Isa 11:10-14), the fulfillment of the promises to David (Jer 23:5-8), promises to the apostles (Matt 19:28), etc. Messiah's return: Matt 23:37-39; Acts 1:9-12; 3:19-21

[39] Jer 31:10

Specifically addressed to the nations, this is a formulation used somewhat infrequently in Scripture. The LORD intends the nations to know that He will regather the same people group He scattered.[40] Believers of all stripes readily acknowledge that the LORD scattered Israel. Fewer are ready to acknowledge His determination to regather Israel, despite the inescapable logic of the text.

The LORD told Abram that He would bring from him a great nation, to whom a specific land was divinely granted.[41] As the covenant is subsequently affirmed to Isaac (not Ishmael) and Jacob (not Esau) we see it function, in the first instance, as a mechanism of *exclusion*.[42] From the outset, however, it is explicit that the LORD will bless *all* families of the earth *through* this unique nation.[43] It is the LORD's prerogative to choose one nation through which to bless (and judge) all nations, and to maintain that distinction throughout history.[44]

---

[40] Israel past, present and future is frequently treated as though there exists a corporate Jewish consciousness, e.g. Zech 12:10 where it is said of future Jews who recognise Messiah, "They will look on me, the one they have pierced…"

[41] Gen 12:1,2,7

[42] Gen 17:19-21; 28:13-15; 35:12

[43] Gen 12:3; 26:4; 28:14; Num 23:9; Deut 32:9; Ps 147:19-20

[44] The radical unity achieved by Jew and non-Jew being one in Messiah (Eph 2:13,14) does not negate national distinctions. See: Part II, *Fallacious Reasoning*

Jacob (renamed Israel) fathered twelve sons from whom descend the tribes of Israel.[45] Biblical genealogies are patrilineal. Thus descent from the three patriarchs via the male line constitutes Jewishness, biblically speaking.[46]

Israel consists of both believers and unbelievers and is seen as a nation and ethnic group with divine covenants, a specific land, and a divine King.[47] Israel was promised a kingdom and has a schedule of geographically located and time referenced prophetic events.[48]

---

[45] Gen 35:10; 49:1-28

[46] • The NT is consistent with this understanding, even to the point of distinguishing between Jews and converts to Judaism, e.g. Acts 2:5,11; 13:43
• It is of course acknowledged that the modern state of Israel has many non-Jewish citizens, including Muslims, Druze and others. This does not contradict the notion of the physical descendants of Abraham, Isaac and Jacob constituting Israel as a nation in perpetuity, as per Jer 31:36: "Only if these decrees vanish from my sight," declares the LORD, "will the descendants of Israel ever cease to be a nation before me."
• Interestingly, Jewishness is today usually treated as matrilineal. Some suggest the change was made as a result of the frequent rape of Jewish women by their non-Jewish persecutors. The change eased the stigma for the resulting children.
• The Cohanim, the priestly line descended from Aaron, are still identified according to patrilineal descent. This is consistent with the predicted future temple(s) requiring men of the correct descent to serve as priests.
• Some Jews downplay ethnic considerations and speak of Jewishness as a religion.

[47] Gen 13:17; 35:12; Isa 9:6,7; Mic 5:2; Luke 1:32,33; Rom 9:4; Heb 11:8,9

[48] Kingdom: 1 Chron 17:11,12; Luke 21:31; 22:18,29,30; Acts 1:3,6
Events include those outlined in Daniel's seventy sevens (Dan 9:24-27), regathering (Ezek 37), invasion (Ezek 38), events of Matt 24.

God promised severe discipline and dispersion for sin but that He would ultimately restore Israel to her divine King and to her land.[49] He will do so *with all His heart and soul*.[50]

WHAT, THEN, IS THE CHURCH?

Paul places a strong emphasis on the concept of being *in Christ* (or *in Messiah*.)[51] He speaks of those who believe in the Messiah being baptised by the Holy Spirit into *one body*.[52] From our perspective it is difficult to grasp just how radical this concept must have seemed in the first century: that both believing Jews and believing non-Jews could be united in a single entity variously described by Paul as *one new man, God's household, a dwelling in which God lives by his Spirit*, and more.[53]

Many dictionaries define *church* as "edifice for public worship", but this is a meaning never used in Scripture. Church *(ekklesia)* has two dominant usages in the New Testament: reference to the *universal* church,[54] consisting of all believers; and the *local* church, typically a congregation.[55]

---

49 Deut 28:15-68; Isa 11:11,12; Hos 3:4,5; Zech 12:10

50 Jer 32:41

51 Note for example the number of times *in Christ* or *in Him* appears in Eph 1. It is by belief one gains such a status (v13).

52 1 Cor 12:13; Gal 3:27

53 Eph 2:15-22

54 e.g. Eph 3:10

55 e.g. 1 Cor 15:19

It is important to observe how *different in kind* the church is, relative to Israel.

In contrast to Israel, the church consists only of believers and it is multi-ethnic.[56] It has no land nor covenants of its own,[57] and is explicitly new.[58]

Messiah is spoken of not as the church's *King* but as its *Head*.[59] Prophecies relating to the church seem to lack specific time and geographical markers.[60]

The church was unrevealed in the Old Testament, was future to Messiah's first coming, and came into existence at Pentecost.[61] Jewish and non-Jew-

---

[56] Of course *local* congregations can include unbelievers but the *universal* church (body of Christ) of 1 Cor 12:13 consists only of believers.
Jewish believers are members both of Israel and the church.

[57] Our citizenship is seen as *in heaven* Phil 3:20. The church enjoys a relationship with, and commemorates the NC, but the covenant is explicitly made with Israel and Judah Jer 31, Heb 8.

[58] Eph 2:15

[59] Eph 5:23; Col 1:18

[60] e.g. Jn 14:1-3; 1 Cor 3:12-15; 1 Thes 4:15-17; 1 Tim 4:1

[61] Matt 16:18; Jn 7:39; Acts 1:5; 1 Cor 12:13. If the giving of the Spirit was subsequent to Messiah's glorification (Jn 7), and if the church is a body into which believers are baptised by the Spirit, then that entity could not have existed prior to Pentecost. The OT was clear that many non-Jews would worship the God of Israel (Isa 19:24; 49:6,7; Mal 1:11), but the concept of the church, in which Jew and non-Jew are united as one on equal terms, was unrevealed in the OT.

ish believers enjoy equal standing in the church.[62] Whereas one is a Jew by birth, it is by the new birth one enters the church.

Non-Jewish believers enjoy Israel's spiritual blessings, are seen as being unnaturally grafted into a tree that belongs to Israel, and are cautioned concerning their attitude toward Jews.[63]

This book will argue that failure to adequately distinguish between the two entities, Israel and the church, is a cause of deep confusion.

---

[62] This was revolutionary and was initially resisted by Jewish believers. Acts 10:9-11:18; 15:1-11; Gal 3:26-29. Non-Jewish believers are sons of Abraham by faith Rom 4:16,17. They are *never* seen as sons of Abraham, Isaac, and Jacob, or as "spiritual Jews".

[63] Eph 3:6; Rom 15:27; Rom 11:17-25

…but in regard to election
they are dearly loved
for the sake of the fathers.
For the gifts and the call of God
are irrevocable.

Romans 11:28-29

3

THINKING BIBLICALLY ABOUT ISRAEL

This relatively short book is an attempt to place Israel correctly in the biblical worldview. It is hoped it will provide some of the foundational tools to enable the reader to answer questions regarding Israel's significance.

The first two chapters sought to establish that Israel occupies a central place in the plan God is outworking on planet earth, and that Messiah's career and identity are inextricably linked to Israel. It is through Israel that Messiah came,[64] and His return to the earth will be strictly geographically

---

64 Rom 9:5; Mic 5:2

situated, as will His kingdom.[65] Messiah's return to earth is conditioned upon His acceptance by His Jewish people, in their own land.[66]

Israel was established to be a blessing to all peoples, and Messiah is the greatest among many blessings thereby bestowed upon the non-Jewish world.[67] We are to stand in right relationship to Israel's Messiah and to Israel.[68]

Nations themselves are a divine institution and Israel stands unique among the nations.[69] Ultimately, those who stand in antagonism toward Israel are seen to fall under God's judgment.[70]

So, should Christians support Israel? An unqualified *yes* can be unhelpful. *Yes* has been too frequently interpreted as granting Israel *carte blanche* in all respects. Rather, the question demands a nuanced response, one that considers historical, geo-

---

[65] Isa 2:1-4; Zech 14:4,9; Matt 23:37-39; 24:15-31; Luke 1:33; 22:18,29,30; Acts 1:3,6

[66] Zech 12:10; Matt 23:39

[67] Gen 12:3b; Isa 49:6; Gal 3:8; Matt 28:19

[68] Gen 12:3; Num 24:9; Jn 3:16; Phil 2:9-11

[69] Nations: Gen 10:4,20,31; Acts 17:26. National entities remain much in view in the future kingdom, e.g. Isa 19:23-25; Zech 8:22,23 Israel's uniqueness: Num 23:9; Deut 7:6; 32:8-9 LXX or ESV; Amos 3:2; Ps 147:19,20; Jer 31:10; Rom 9:4,5

[70] This is a significant prophetic theme, e.g. Ezek 35:5-9; 36:5-7; Joel 3:1-3; Obad 10,15; Matt 25:31-46

political, legal and ethical factors,[71] while always allowing Scripture to function as the final authority.

In their enthusiasm, Israel's Christian supporters can sometimes claim modern Israel as fulfillment of certain prophecies that clearly remain unfulfilled.[72] This is equally unhelpful.

THE ABSTRACT JEW

Unhelpful too, is the phenomenon within certain Christian streams that tends to reduce the Jewish people to an abstraction. The Jews are seen as central players in a future cosmic scenario but are granted minimal relevance and significance in the

---

[71] For commentary on historical, geo-political, legal and ethical matters relating to Israel:
What Should We Think About Israel?, Randall Price (editor)
https://www.thinc.info/
https://israelinstitute.nz/
https://honestreporting.com/

[72] Dozens of unfulfilled prophecies could be cited. In the first few chapters of Isaiah alone, a few of the predictions that have clearly *not* been fulfilled by present day Israel are Isa 1:25-2:5; 3:18-4:6; 11:4-16. And of course the New covenant promise that [those of *the house of Israel and the house of Judah*] *shall all know me* (Jer 31:31,34) has not been fulfilled.

present.[73] Of course, a people group reduced to a theological abstraction makes few demands, and for some, that is certainly preferable, more palatable and convenient.[74] Unlike the modern state of Israel and the real flesh and blood Jews of the here and now, an abstraction imposes no obligations and presents far fewer complexities with which to contend.[75]

THE BETTER QUESTION

So, back in the real world, the better question to

---

[73] Jewish commentators have noted this phenomenon. For example, Gershom: "They're seeing the Jews as actors in a Christian drama leading toward the end of days." https://www.npr.org/2008/05/16/90509127/an-israeli-journalists-take-on-christian-zionism
While Gershom may be correct in observing Christians reducing Jews to "actors", it is incorrect to imply that it is only Christians who place the Jewish people in a pivotal role in the end of days. The central role played by the Jews in the present and future is comprehensively articulated in the Hebrew Scriptures and in rabbinic writings.

[74] Such an attitude is frequently a consequence of the belief that the Jews have been *temporarily set aside*. This view is popular even among those who affirm a future restoration of Israel. However, the Scriptures teach that *Israel has experienced a hardening in part until the full number of the Gentiles has come in (Rom 11:25),* an entirely different concept. See further comments in footnotes of Chapter 6.

[75] A similar phenomenon exists within the field of Holocaust memorialisation. Many are ready to commemorate dead Jews and to inappropriately universalise the lessons of the Holocaust in service of current social justice issues. Fewer are ready to recognise that the forces that inspired and facilitated the Holocaust are alive and well today and are a direct threat to living Jews and to Israel, the state of the Jews. On universalisation see:
https://holocaustfoundation.com/universalisation
https://holocaustfoundation.com/blog/2019/8/7/saving-the-shoah-a-brief-survey-of-denial-and-distortion

ask is, *What is the biblical significance of modern Israel?*

Israel's recent regathering and present condition is certainly consistent with a number of biblical predictions.[76] Further, some argue from Isaiah 11 that mention of a *second international* regathering in the context of Israel's final restoration necessarily implies a *first international* regathering.[77] If that is the case, then it can be stated with confidence that the present regathering is biblically significant.

The argument is further strengthened by a number of predictions that clearly require a national regathering, largely in unbelief, prior to there being a fulfillment.[78]

---

[76] Including Ezek 36:24-25; Zeph 2:1-2 The famous dry bones prophecy of Ezek 37 sets out a specific order of events for *the whole house of Israel* (v11). The bones *came together* in v7 and 8 but only subsequently *the breath came into them* (v9,10).

[77] This argument is made by Fruchtenbaum:
http://www.arielcontent.org/dcs/pdf/mbs189m.pdf
Hungarian Hebrew Christian Adolf Saphir, 1831-1891, taught there would be two international regatherings.
Also, Nicholson, about 70 years prior to 1948, "believed that there would be two phases to the return: a return in unbelief and a return with national belief in process." *Forsaking Israel, 2nd addition p373, Kindle.*
Thus, this view was not the invention of 20th century American prophecy teachers.

[78] e.g. Zech 12:1-10; Matt 24:14-31; 2 Thes 2:4; Rev 11:1-13

Thinking Biblically:
A Thought Experiment

Israel is subject to more condemnation at the United Nations than all other nations combined.[79] If we form our views of Israel based on the utterances of mainstream media,[80] the United Nations, Amnesty International,[81] and even some ostensibly evangelical[82] institutions, we might conclude that Israel is an apartheid state, a settler colonialist project, and an occupier of Palestinian indigenous lands.[83] These are serious charges and demand careful examination. While it is not the burden of

---

[79] https://tinyurl.com/ycychc2t
https://unwatch.org/database/

[80] https://tinyurl.com/5y96mm7x
https://tinyurl.com/ywynswp9

[81] https://tinyurl.com/6kvb9acw
https://tinyurl.com/j6vd4f43

[82] It is acknowledged that the definition of *evangelical* is contested. (e.g. *Four Views on the Spectrum of Evangelicalism*, Zondervan, 2011). Throughout this volume the author is primarily using the term as reference to those Christians who claim to hold Scripture as authoritative.

[83] Emeritus Prof Dov Bing: 'The Arabs have never had a name for this country. "Filastin" is the Arabic transliteration of Palestine, the name the Romans gave the country when they determined to obliterate the presence of the Jewish people. The researchers of the archaeologist Edward Robinson revealed that hundreds of place-names of villages and sites, seemingly Arab, were Arabic renderings or transliterations of ancient Hebrew names, biblical or Talmudic... ... Palestine was never an exclusively Arab country. There was never a separate Palestinian Arab nation. Palestinian nationalism is a post-World War I phenomenon.' https://tinyurl.com/5dz3k4m6

the present volume, it can be said that all these charges can be demonstrated to be false.[84]

For argument's sake, however, let us assume that all such charges are entirely true - that these accusations and worse are all well grounded. Should this undermine or annul the biblical data concerning Israel's present and future status?

Let us take our thought experiment further: imagine we lived in the period of Jeremiah and witnessed his announcement of the New covenant, a covenant explicitly made with the house of Israel and the house of Judah.[85] The covenant promises national redemption,[86] restoration to the land,[87] transformed hearts and minds,[88] a righteous King ruling in their midst,[89] national perpetuity,[90] and more.

The challenge is this: these promises were made while Judah was deep in apostasy, and had been engaging in idol worship and even child

---

[84] https://tinyurl.com/2p8ybr3m
https://www.thinc.info
https://tinyurl.com/2ux7vf4v
https://www.indigenouscoalition.org/articles-blog/full-interview-with-yoseph-haddad
[85] Jer 31:31; Heb 8:8
[86] Jer 33:6-9
[87] Jer 32:37-41
[88] Jer 31:33,34
[89] Jer 33:15,16
[90] Jer 31:35-37; 33:25,26

sacrifice.[91] Surely, in the time of Jeremiah we would have struggled to reconcile the solemn and unambiguous divine declarations of the New covenant with the reality on the ground. These are such gracious promises to such an undeserving people!

Similarly, today it takes mental discipline to develop a nuanced yet biblical view of Israel within a culture that is deeply hostile (and within a church that increasingly submits to culture rather than to Scripture).

Arguably, thinking biblically about Israel is more difficult than thinking biblically about the various cultural and moral norms increasingly under attack in modern society. Not only is much of mainstream media and the present culture hostile to the world's only Jewish state, but we must also contend with at least seventeen centuries of aberrant Christian theology concerning the Jewish people, and the antisemitism that has tragically flowed from that theology.[92]

---

[91] Jer 7:30-31

[92] Addressed in Chapter 5 and Part II. Also, an introduction to the issue (a short film series): https://www.evangelicalzionism.com Christian theology was an important factor in preparing the ground for the Holocaust, see Chapters 7 and 8. See also Michael Brown's *Our Hands Are Stained With Blood: The Tragic Story of the "Church" and the Jewish People*

Ultimately, antagonism toward the Jewish people and the Jewish state proves to be confirmatory of the biblical data rather than contradictory. If we take seriously what the Bible teaches concerning the spiritual dimension, the degree to which the world is presently under the enemy's control,[93] and the way in which Satan aligns himself against God's purposes, then hatred of the Jewish state (and antisemitism more generally) serve as strong evidence of the Scriptures' veracity.

---

[93] Eph 2:2; 6:12; 1 Jn 5:19 See Chapter 9, *Antisemitism and Its Unseen Cause*

*To them belong
the adoption as sons, the glory,
the covenants…*

Romans 9:4

4

THE
SIGNIFICANCE
OF THE
BIBLICAL
COVENANTS

Theologians vary widely in their approach to the covenants.[94] Some posit theological covenants that are difficult or impos-

---

[94] A working definition: a solemn and formalised undertaking binding one or both parties to the fulfillment of its content, in accordance with its wording.

sible to find in Scripture.[95] Others speak of up to eight covenants and still others recognise only those explicitly framed and named as covenants.[96] This brief chapter will mention five explicit biblical covenants. Taken at face value, these provide a definite framework for past, present and future history.

The special significance of biblical covenants is evidenced by:

- their formality;[97]
- the oaths God included in the covenants' wording;

---

[95] e.g. Covenant theologian Ligon Duncan acknowledges the existence of the biblical covenants and yet proceeds to justify his embrace of covenants that are not named in Scripture. He rejects the label replacement theology and insists that his view is fulfillment theology. (See Chapter 5, *Replacement Theology*).
https://rts.edu/resources/what-are-some-misconceptions-about-covenant-theology/
Covenant Theology typically argues there are two or three covenants: *grace, works, redemption*. See Henebury's multipart critique:
https://tinyurl.com/yc2etr9r

[96] e.g. Fruchtenbaum sees eight covenants:
http://www.dailyqt.org/docs/eightcovenants_fruchtenbaum.pdf
Henebury sees six "covenants of God." *The Words of the Covenant,* p106. Kindle.
In addition to the five covenants discussed in this chapter, the present author is inclined to recognise distinct divine covenants in Deut 29:1 and Num 25:12,13.

[97] Perhaps the nearest analogy in present day culture is the formality of the marriage ceremony. Most choose to gather family and friends as important witnesses to formal marriage oaths; follow a degree of ritual to further emphasise the solemnity of the undertakings made; and use rings as symbols of the commitment.

- the extended treatment given to the covenants by biblical writers;
- their repeated reference in later Scripture.

NOAH

Scripture's first mention of *covenant* is in reference to God's covenant with Noah.[98] While the covenant's content is not without implications for the topic of Israel, it is its treatment by theologians and Bible readers that is most illuminating for our present purposes.[99]

The Noahic covenant's meaning is little contested and is usually taken as read by conservatives.[100] The covenant is not restated in the New Testament and we are aware of no-one who suggests that it *must* be restated in order for its terms and intentions to remain valid. Thus the Noahic covenant passes largely unscathed into Christian understanding.[101]

---

[98] Gen 6:18 In fact the covenant is made with Noah, all mankind and every living creature thereafter. Gen 9:12

[99] Gen 9:26,27 Translators differ as to whether it is God or Japheth who will *dwell in the tents of Shem* (v27). The implications for the issue of Israel are notable either way.

[100] Theistic evolutionists contest the extent of the flood, and others, the identity of the Nephilim. But these are not the content of the covenant. Seldom contested are the parties to the covenant, terms, territory, tenure.

[101] '…this first covenant is interpreted uniformly in what we call a "literal" way.' Henebury, *The Words of the Covenant*, p240, Kindle.

In contrast, it is the later covenants made with Israel that are subject to denial or reinterpretation at the hands of many theologians.[102]

ABRAHAM

God's covenant with Abram (later Abraham) appears immediately following the Genesis account of the divine establishment of distinct nations.[103] The covenant announcement sets out God's promise to establish an additional nation, later to be referred to as Israel, *foremost among the nations,* His *firstborn.*[104]

Genesis 12
1. Now the LORD said to Abram, "Go forth from your country, and from your relatives and from your father's house, to the land which I will show you;
2. And I will make you a great nation, and I will bless you, and make your name great; and so you shall be a blessing;
3. And I will bless those who bless you, and the one who curses you I will curse. And in you all the families of the earth will be blessed...

---

[102] Later covenants are subjected to allegorisation, spiritualization, neo-Marcionism, redefinition, etc. Issues of materiality (promises of land, descent, regathering, physical security) seem to suffer most, and yet texts relating to Israel's curses *are* taken as read.

[103] Gen 10 and 11. Being one of the divine institutions, nations remain very much in view in the NT and the prophetic future (Acts 17:26; Zech 8:23).

[104] Ex 4:22; Jer 31:7
The *content* of the covenant was announced in Gen 12 but the covenant was established in Gen 15.

7. ... The LORD appeared to Abram and said, "To your descendants I will give this land."

This foundational passage uses the word *bless* or *blessing* five times in just two verses. Though the word *curse* is also used, it is described as reactive on God's part: those who curse Abraham or his people will be cursed by God.[105] In the Hebrew two different words are used, further strengthening the principle. This is reflected in the NET rendition:

... but the one who treats you lightly I must curse.

The covenant is made with Abraham, his son Isaac (Ishmael is excluded), and Isaac's son Jacob (Esau is excluded).[106] Thus, the covenant is unambiguously narrow and exclusionary in establishing the foundation of one particular nation. And yet the covenant is simultaneously universal in the applicability of blessing: blessing is promised to *all the families of the earth*.[107]

The status of God's covenant with Abraham as a major biblical landmark is seen in multiple ways:

---

[105] Gen 12:2,3
Verse 2 addresses Abram and his nation. Verse 3 establishes: 1. the divine policy concerning Israel and the non-Jewish world
(Num 24:9; Joel 3:1-3; Ezek 36:5-8; Matt 25:31-46)
2. the universal applicability of blessing (Gal 3:8), even though the *vehicle* is narrowly defined
[106] Gen 17:18-21; 28:13-15; 35:10-12; 1 Chr 16:15-18; Ps 105:8-11
[107] Gen 12:3. See Chapter 2.

- two thousand years of biblical history is covered in summary form until mention of Abram (Abraham) and his covenant. Thereafter the pace of Genesis slows dramatically. One particular family line comes into focus and its history is dealt with in great detail;

- the content of God's covenant with Abraham is repeatedly restated;[108]

- God's decision to formalise this matter with a covenantal oath gives it great weight;[109]

- references to the covenant are numerous in both Testaments.[110]

Remarkably, God binds Himself to the covenant's fulfillment while preventing Abraham from doing so.[111]

Attempts to downplay the covenantal land grant to Abraham and his nation are common, but

---

[108] Gen 13:14-17; 15:7,8,18-21; 17:8; 24:7; 26:3,4; 28:4,13; 35:12; 48:4; 50:24; Ex 6:4,8 etc

[109] Gen 24:7; Heb 6:13-17

[110] e.g. Ex 2:24; 6:4-8; Dt 10:11; 34:4; Neh 9:8; Ps 105:44; Jer 32:22; Ezek 20:42; Luke 1:55,72,73; Acts 3:25;7:5; Rom 9:4;15:8; Heb 11:9

[111] Gen 15:8-18 It is likely a self-maledictory oath. Thus its ultimate fulfillment is not conditional upon Abraham's performance.

should be resisted. That the land is a central and essential covenant component is clear.[112]

Moses

The divine covenant mediated by Moses was bilateral and conditional, promising blessing for obedience and severe punishment (including expulsion) for disobedience.[113] The covenant was made between God and the people of Israel.[114] At the same time it had, and has, multiple other functions.[115] Later, the prophet Jeremiah is to speak of the Mosaic covenant as *broken*.[116]

Several prophetic passages appear in association with the Mosaic covenant, setting out Israel's inevitable failure, punishment, dispersion and distress, but also her ultimate restoration.[117] A clear historical outline is thus established.

---

[112] Gen 13:17 negates attempts to spiritualize the land promise (also Deut 34:4). The land becomes the stage for Messiah's first and second advent and the pivotal events of biblical history.

[113] Blessing: Deut 28:1-14 Punishment: Deut 28:16-58; 32:19-35

[114] Ex 19:1-7; Deut 4:13,14. It was not made with the non-Jewish world.
In addition, the establishment of the Mosaic covenant did not set aside the Abrahamic covenant Gal 3:17.

[115] Among these: maintaining Israel's separation from the pagan nations; regulating her national life and worship; acting as a tutor to lead to Messiah (Gal 3:19,24); making sin more sinful (thus emphasising the need of a saviour Rom 7:14); etc.

[116] Jer 31:32

[117] Deut 4:27-31; 30:1-7; Lev 26:14-45
Judgement: Deut 32:19-35
Restoration: Deut 32:36-43

DAVID

King David is promised a royal lineage and that he will never lack a descendant eligible to sit upon his throne.[118] There will be one particular descendant whose throne and kingdom will endure forever and Israel will one day enjoy freedom from oppression.[119] Elsewhere we learn that this predicted ruler of Israel, who becomes known as the Son of David, will be of eternal origin.[120]

The Davidic covenant builds on earlier predictions of a worthy conquering ruler, a descendant of Judah, one who will ultimately destroy Israel's enemies and bring peace.[121] The gospels' frequent use of the term *Son of David* signals the prophetically inspired expectation that existed at the time of Messiah's first coming.[122]

NEW

The New covenant is announced at a very low point in Israel's history when she is in a state of deep national apostasy. It is at the outset contrasted with the *broken* Mosaic covenant.[123] The New Testament also emphasises the superiority and dis-

---

[118] Jer 33:17
[119] 1 Chr 17:11-14; Ps 89:3,4;132:11; Jer 30:20-22
[120] Isa 9:6,7(5,6); Mic 5:2
[121] Gen 49:8-12; Num 24:17-19
[122] e.g. Matt 12:23; 20:30; 22:42-45; Luke 1:32-33 etc.
[123] Jer 31:31-34

similarity of the New covenant relative to the Mosaic.[124]

Forgiveness of sin and internal transformation, elsewhere shown to be by means of the Holy Spirit, are promised to the Jewish people.[125] Also associated with the New covenant are the regathering of the Jews, national restoration and the establishment of the kingdom.[126]

The New covenant appears to bring together and enable elements of earlier covenants.[127]

Interestingly, the promised Messiah is Himself referred to by the term *covenant*.[128] Presumably, this is because He is ultimately the covenant maker, *the messenger of the covenant*, and the once-for-all sacrifice by which the covenant is made.[129]

Centuries later the Messiah is rejected by most of His own people at His first coming, *as predicted* by

---

[124] 2 Cor 3:7-16; Heb 8:6,7,13 The New is not a renewal of the Mosaic.

[125] Jer 31:33,34; Ezek 36:26; 37:14; Zech 12:10-13:1; Isa 44:3

[126] Ezek 36:24,28; Jer 33:14-26

[127] Particularly provisions of the Abrahamic and Davidic covenants but also certain things promised in the writings of Moses e.g. Deut 30:4-6.

[128] Isa 42;6; 49:8

[129] Mal 3:1; Heb 10:12-16

Isaiah.[130] Nonetheless, the New covenant is inaugurated.[131]

The provisions of the New covenant are seen to inform the expectations and hope of New Testament believers.[132]

Subsequent to Israel's rejection of Messiah, she is in the present period spoken of as *hardened in part*.[133] The covenantally promised restoration awaits her future acceptance of Messiah.[134] In the interim, non-Jewish believers enjoy *riches* and *reconciliation* and find themselves *unnaturally grafted* into a tree belonging to Israel.[135]

SUMMARY

Thus, even this brief survey of five biblical covenants lays a foundation and specific framework by which later revelation can be better understood. The covenants contribute to a sense of our place in unfolding biblical history and the

---

[130] Isa 49:6,7; 53:1-4 Though rejected by the national leadership, Messiah was accepted by a significant minority of Jews.

[131] Luke 22:20; 1 Cor 11:25 Many of its provisions remain unfulfilled till Messiah's return e.g. universal knowledge of the Lord amongst the Jewish people Jer 31:34; Heb 8:11.

[132] As does content from Abrahamic and Davidic covenants. Matt 19:28; Luke 1:32,33;70-74; 2:25;38; 24:21; Acts 1:3,6; 26:6,7; Rom 11:25-27; 15:8

[133] Rom 11:15 speaks of Israel's rejection of Messiah, not the inverse (Rom 11:1) Rom 11:25; 2 Cor 3:14-16

[134] Rom 11:26,27; Acts 3:19-21

[135] Rom 11:12 Riches especially include the gift of the Holy Spirit. Rom 11:15,24

times in which we live.

The land promised to Abraham and his descendants is the stage on which pivotal biblical events take place.[136] Understanding Israel's future destiny (and that of her King) helps us develop not only a sound view of Israel in her present state, but also the church's place in the divine plan.

---

[136] Past and future. Thus the highly contested status of Israel (and Jerusalem in particular), geopolitically and theologically.

The word of the LORD
came to Jeremiah:
Have you not noticed that
these people are saying,
'The LORD has rejected
the two kingdoms he chose'?

So they despise my people
and no longer regard them
as a nation.

Jeremiah 33:23-24

5

REPLACEMENT THEOLOGY

What is replacement theology? A number of theologians have offered robust definitions of replacement theology or supersessionism.[137] While it varies in its expression, terminology and justification, replacement theology always includes the concept that the church (or Jesus) has in some way displaced, replaced, superseded, disenfranchised, redefined, or fulfilled Israel and/or Israel's biblical status and covenantal promises.

According to Walter C. Kaiser:

Replacement theology, then, declared that the Church, Abraham's spiritual seed, had replaced national Israel in that it had transcended and fulfilled

---

[137] The two terms are used interchangeably.
Vlach includes within this article his own definition plus those of Soulen and Ridderbos: https://tinyurl.com/une6cvv7
Diprose's definition (quoted by Ice): https://tinyurl.com/ycypu57y

the terms of the covenant given to Israel, which covenant Israel had lost because of disobedience.[138]

IS IT FAIR TO USE THE TERM "REPLACEMENT THEOLOGY"?

Interestingly, many of those who hold to replacement theology have been strident in their objection to the use of the term.[139] Rather than *replacement theology*, some insist that their view is in

---

[138] Kaiser's *An Assessment of "Replacement Theology"*: https://tinyurl.com/m99r69fa
There appears to be typo in the online version of Kaiser's piece [(dis)obedience]. Nonetheless, it offers a useful critique, summarised thus: "1) The "New Covenant" was made with the house of Israel and Judah. God never made a formal covenant with the Church; 2) The failure of the Jews, like the failure of the Church, was calculated in the plan of God (Rom 11:8); 3) The New Testament clearly teaches that God has not cast off disobedient Israel (Rom 11:1,25-26), for they are the natural branches into which the Church has been grafted; 4) The "eternal" aspect of the promise of the land is not to be equated with the "eternal" aspect of the Aaronic priesthood (I Chr 23:13) or the Rechabite descendants (Jer 35:19); and 5) Paul's allegory of Galatians 4:21-31 does not teach that national Israel has been replaced by the Church; it teaches that the quest for justification by works leads to bondage whereas justification by faith and grace leads to freedom and salvation."

[139] Vlach responds: 'We find it somewhat hollow for some to argue against the title "replacement theology" when replacement terminology has often been used by those who believe the church is the new or true Israel.' ... 'Those who argue for "fulfillment," "enlargement," "expansion," and/or "transference" language do not use different arguments than those who argue for "replacement."' Mishkan, Vol 65, 2010, pp 28-42. An explanation for the indignation is offered here: https://tinyurl.com/yeympafu

fact *expansion*,[140] *extension*,[141] *fulfillment*,[142] *inclusion*,[143] or *completion*[144] theology. It may be granted that proponents of a position have a right to name that position as they see fit. However, labels such as these prompt certain obvious questions.

- How is it that in *expansion* or *extension theology*, the major portion of the original structure is neither expanded nor extended, but rather demolished?

- How is it that in *fulfillment theology*, the numerous explicit national promises to Israel will never be fulfilled?

- How is it that in *inclusion theology*, Israel's God-sworn national and territorial promises are explicitly excluded?

- How is it that in *completion theology*, Messiah's mission and the divinely covenanted programme for Israel will never be completed?[145]

---

[140] e.g. https://pastorjoev.wordpress.com/2016/01/08/replacement-theology-or-expansion-theology/
https://www.monergism.com/not-replacement-expansion
[141] e.g. https://fliphtml5.com/yvii/wtvr/basic
Also, *The Gospel and the Land of Promise: Christian Approaches to the Land of the Bible*, p153. Authored mostly by Laidlaw College and Carey Baptist College writers. Hereafter GLP.
[142] e.g. https://rts.edu/resources/what-are-some-misconceptions-about-covenant-theology/
[143] e.g. https://www.samstorms.org/enjoying-god-blog/post/replacement-theology-or-inclusion-theology
[144] Parsons references *completion theology*:
https://www.hebrew4christians.com/Articles/Christendom/christendom.html#loaded
[145] For Messiah's mission, see *Appendix: Messianic Prophecy*

The reader may make his or her own judgement as to whether such terms are merely euphemisms.

Ultimately, how replacement theology is named is less important than what it teaches.

IN THEIR OWN WORDS

Replacement theologians make a range of affirmations. Typical are the following:

The Jewish nation no longer has a place as the special people of God; that place has been taken by the Christian community which fulfills God's purpose for Israel.[146]

The community of believers has in all respects replaced carnal, national Israel. …the Israel of the Old Testament (so called 'Racial Israel') had been replaced by the Israel of the New Testament, the Christian Church.[147]

We Christians can not speak of the 'promised land' as an exclusive right for a privileged Jewish people. This promise was nullified by Christ. There is no longer a chosen people — all men and women of all countries have become the chosen people.[148]

---

[146] Bruce Waltke, quoted in *Three Views on Israel and the Church,* p22 (fn)

[147] Respectively, Herman Bavinck, Reformed Dogmatics, 4.667 and Charles Povan, both quoted by Henebury: https://tinyurl.com/2zvz7enx His series includes many such quotes.

[148] Bustros: https://www.jpost.com/International/Vatican-synod-calls-for-end-to-Israels-occupation

The church, according to the New Testament, is the eschatological Israel incorporated in Jesus Messiah… What was promised to Israel has now been fulfilled in the church, in Christ, especially the Spirit and the new covenant…[149]

Whoever believes in Jesus is the true Israel…   The church is the expansion of Israel.[150]

Whether one uses *expansion, fulfillment, inclusion, extension, completion, replacement* or some other term to describe this view, its detrimental impact on the biblical worldview is the same. The primary issues come into sharp focus when one considers what replacement theology *denies.*

Replacement theology denies the ultimate literal fulfillment of Scripture's numerous plainly stated declarations and refer-ences**[151] **concerning Israel's national re-demption, restoration and regathering to her ancestral lands, along with the estab-lishment of her kingdom with Messiah ruling from Jerusalem.[152]

---

[149] *Dictionary of Biblical Prophecy and End Times,* Hays, Duvall, Pate p330
[150] https://youtu.be/1Ua3CP0zJ2E   Though this video is short it manages to misconstrue at least six biblical passages.
[151] References to Israel's restoration, in the book of Isaiah *alone,* include: 1:26,27; 2:1-5; 4:2-6; 9:7; 10:20-27; 11:6-16; 14:1,2; 19:23-25; 24:23; 26:6-9; 27:6,12,13; 33:17-24; 35:10; 40:1-11; 43:5,6; 49:8-26; 51:11; 52:1-12; 54:10-16; 56:6-8; 60:3-22; 61:4-11; 62:1-12; 65:17-25; 66:10-20.
[152] Denial of Israel's prophesied future necessarily entails distortion of her present status.

Replacement theology began to appear in the second century. It is obvious in the writings of Justin Martyr, 100-165:

For the true spiritual Israel... ...are we who have been led to God through this crucified Christ.[153]

Origen, 185-254, was a brilliant scholar and a significant figure in advancing an allegorical understanding of the Scriptures. He promoted a three tier interpretive scheme paralleling body, soul and spirit.[154] The body corresponded to the lowest and least significant meaning of a text: its plain, literal meaning. The higher meanings were the soulish and the spiritual.

While Origen was excommunicated on more than one occasion, his contribution to the decline of biblical understanding was significant. His replacement theology was explicit:

We may thus assert in utter confidence that the Jews will not return to their earlier situation, for they have committed the most abominable of crimes... ...and another people was called by God to the blessed election.[155]

---

[153] https://www.ccel.org/ccel/schaff/anf01.viii.iv.xi.html The unbridled allegorisation of Origen c.185-253 was an important further development.

[154] "For as man consists of body, and soul, and spirit, so in the same way does Scripture." https://tinyurl.com/h8jpjyzf

[155] History of Antisemitism: https://tinyurl.com/mw8mp7p7

While in his lifetime there had been resistance to Origen's allegorical approach, it eventually became well established in the church.

The influence of Augustine, 354-430, can not be overstated, both in terms of Christian thought generally and supersessionism in particular.[156]

…we are Israel, the seed of Abraham… …Let therefore no Christian consider himself alien to the name of Israel.[157]

…indeed, Judas is the image of the Jewish people.[158]

Contempt for the Jews, an allegorical approach to the Scriptures and identification of the church as the new Israel did not originate with Augustine. However, the way that Augustine was revered in subsequent centuries meant such ideas became deeply entrenched in Christian thought.[159] The biblical texts relating to the restoration of Israel were destined to be ignored, allegorised or distorted by much of Christendom for many centuries.

---

[156] Augustine's ideas "dominated the medieval debate" according to Hood, quoted here: https://tinyurl.com/y3xwnv8s
See also Vlach: https://freerepublic.com/focus/f-religion/3160106/posts

[157] https://ccel.org/ccel/schaff/npnf108/npnf108.ii.CXIV.html

[158] *The Anguish of the Jews,* Flannery, p52

[159] While there is much more to replacement theology than eschatology, Augustine's shift from premillennialism to amillennialism was very significant. See Anderson: https://faithalone.org/wp-content/uploads/2020/04/anderson.pdf

Despite the loud and indignant protests to the contrary, most churches embrace some form of replacement theology. Anglican Canon Andrew White concurs:

Almost all the Churches hold to replacement theology.[160]

The relationship between replacement theology and antisemitism must be articulated carefully. It is to be emphasised that replacementists are not necessarily antisemitic. According to Vlach:

...replacement theology has often been linked with anti-Semitism in history. Not all who hold to a replacement view are anti-Semitic, but history is littered with atrocities committed against the Jewish people when the church overwhelmingly adopts replacement theology and has an influence on society.[161]

Melanie Philips speaks of replacement theology as *key in fanning the flames of the Holocaust, which could not have happened without 2,000 years of anti-Jewish polemic...*[162]

---

[160] At the time Canon of Coventry Cathedral and the Archbishop of Canterbury's representative in the Middle East.

[161] *What Should We Think About Israel?*, loc 3014, Kindle.

[162] http://archive.spectator.co.uk/article/16th-february-2002/14/christians-who-hate-the-jews

HOW DOES REPLACEMENT THEOLOGY ARGUE ITS CASE?

What follows is a brief survey of some of the concepts and characteristics of replacement theology.[163] These are more easily understood when illustrated with examples from the writings of supersessionists themselves. In the interest of this chapter's brevity, each of the following is elaborated upon, with examples, in Part II, *Turning The Text On Its Head.*

1. REINTERPRETATION

Key terms and concepts are said to be reinterpreted and redefined by New Testament writers. Once accepted as legitimate, reinterpretation can be used to overturn any Old Testament or New Testament statement or concept.

2. PROOF TEXTING AND DECONTEXTUALISATION

Certain key texts are cited out of context and misinterpreted. By this means, a few lines of text are used to effectively annul explicit covenantal promises and large volumes of biblical data.

---

[163] A tentative taxonomy, which makes no claim to being exhaustive. Many of these strategies overlap, or are employed simultaneously.

3. Neo-Marcionism

The Old Testament text is granted less authority than the New Testament or is simply ignored. Replacement theology's interpretation of the New Testament becomes the lens through which Old Testament texts must be understood.

4. Typology, Allegory and Spiritualization

Israel is reduced to mere symbols, metaphors or shadows of some future superior reality, typically the church or Jesus. Texts describing Israel's future are said to denote present spiritual realities.

5. Christological Interpretation

Christ is employed as the lens through which Israel's covenantal promises are reinterpreted. First, He must be ethnically cleansed, de-Judaised and otherwise misrepresented before He is useful to the supersessionists as a (re)interpretative lens.

6. Conflation and "Amorphization"

Biblical concepts are stripped of their particularity and detail so as to achieve an amorphous generality. Thereby Israel's covenantal uniqueness is denied and Messiah's identity distorted.

7. Fallacious Reasoning

Assertions are made that do not follow from the biblical data.

8. Theological Override

A theological framework or motif is presupposed, to which all biblical data must submit. Having embraced a system of theology, that system becomes the authoritative lens through which all biblical data is read.

WHY SHOULD REPLACEMENT THEOLOGY BE OPPOSED?

The issue of Israel is often portrayed as a peripheral matter, merely a disagreement among Christians over future events. In fact, it directly impacts a central theme in the biblical narrative and has far reaching implications.

- Replacement theology severs the link between divine statement and divine action, prediction and fulfillment.[164] By Scripture's own definition it renders the Old Testament prophets false prophets.[165] Thus replacement theology undermines the coherence and self-authentication of Scripture.

- Replacement theology denigrates God's ability to communicate (and man's God-given ability to understand.) God's words concerning the tree and the serpent and Eve's distortion thereof tell us much about how God communicates:[166]

---

[164] Num 23:19; Isa 46:10; 48:14

[165] Dt 18:22 For such a formula to be coherent there must be a fixed and identifiable connection between prediction and fulfillment. RT's assertion that such expectations are subverted negates OT validation of the NT.

[166] Gen 2:16,17; 3:1-4

He expects His words to be understood and there are consequences for misrepresenting His intentions. The implications for replacement theology are far from trivial.

- Replacement theology warps our understanding of Messiah's offices and return to earth, for which Israel's partial regathering is a prerequisite.[167] Thus replacement theology distorts Messiah's identity and destiny, and our understanding of the future kingdom.[168]

- Replacement theology renders impossible the formation of an accurate and comprehensive worldview, thus leaving the present day believer vulnerable. It has significant implications for the believer's understanding of the present and past, not merely the future.[169] Creationists have correctly argued that a sound view of the past (origins) is essential to a robust Christian faith. Similarly, the biblical data concerning the past, present and future can be thought of, or analo-

---

[167] See *Appendix: Messianic Prophecy*

[168] Zech 12,14; Mic 4:1-8; Mt 24:3-21; Acts 1:3,6

[169] Denial of the ultimate national restoration of Israel helps pave the way for aberrant ideas as diverse as preterism, postmillennialism, amillennialism, reconstructionism, dominionism, Seventh Day Adventism, Christian nationalism, paedobaptism and many more. If it is true that the restoration of Israel is a central and essential biblical theme, then it follows that distortion or denial of that theme will result in theological chaos. Conversely, those groups affirming a restorationist position tend to have much common ground in their understanding of the unfolding of present and future history.

gised, as a journey. Seen in that way, it must be recognised that the destination is certainly no less important than the origin.

- Replacement theology has severely damaged the church's relationship with the Jewish people. While antisemitism does not of necessity always flow from replacement theology, historically it has done so. History is replete with tragic examples.[170]

- Replacement theology renders Messiah unrecognisable to His own people. Among the primary reasons cited by religious Jews for rejection of Jesus' messianic claim, are His apparent failure to regather all dispersed Jews and enforce a kingdom of universal peace.[171] Indeed, if Jesus does not *ultimately* complete both tasks He will indeed have failed in the messianic mission. While this volume holds that Jesus will fulfill such tasks upon His return (along with all remaining messianic prophecies), replacement theology has no coherent and credible response to such objections.

---

[170] Brown's *Our Hands Are Stained With Blood: The Tragic Story of the Church and the Jewish People* provides a disturbing summary of the church's engagement with the Jewish people.
See also Flannery's *Constantine's Sword.*
RT was an important factor in preparing the ground for the Holocaust.
See Chapters 7 and 8
[171] e.g. *Twenty-Six Reasons Why Jews Don't Believe in Jesus*, Norman, p61-62

- Replacement theology is a direct expression of the very hubris (specifically *boasting, arrogance, ignorance* and *conceit*) that Paul warned his readers against, in their consideration of the Jewish people.[172]

- Replacement theology is a slight upon God's honour and His covenant keeping character.[173]

Conversely, there is great blessing along with illumination and clarification, individually and corporately, in developing a biblical view of Israel and seeking to outwork an attitude of blessing toward the Jewish people.[174]

[172] Rom 11:18,20,25 See Chapter 7, *Response and Responsibility*
[173] Jer 32:37-41; 33:25,26; Heb 6:16,17
[174] Gen 12:3

*Now the Bereans
were of more noble character
than the Thessalonians,
for they received the message
with great eagerness
and examined the Scriptures
every day to see
if what Paul said was true.*

Acts 17:11

6

NEW TESTAMENT ASSUMPTIONS AND EXPECTATIONS

T he assertion is often made that the cross, the resurrection and Pentecost changed everything. Indeed, many things *were* radically changed.[175] Distinguishing between those things that were taken out of the way and those that continue, is crucial in forming a biblical view of Israel. Confusion quickly arises when believers

---

[175] Some of the many changes: When Messiah died, the second temple's curtain was torn from top to bottom. The Mosaic sacrificial system was made obsolete (Rom 7:6; Heb 8:13). The dividing wall of partition between Jews and non-Jews was abolished enabling the creation of an entirely *new* entity, the ekklesia or one new man (Eph 2:14-18). The Holy Spirit was given, so that all believers experience His indwelling.

conflate matters that the Scriptures are careful to keep distinct.[176]

Messiah came in fulfillment of detailed and specific Old Testament predictions[177] and the New Testament demonstrates that faithful believers continued to hold the expectation of Israel's ultimate regathering and restoration.

The gospel of Luke reveals much concerning believers' expectations at the time of Jesus' first coming:

- The angel Gabriel, no less, informed Mary that her child would be the promised son of David, destined to rule the Jewish nation.[178]

- Mary's later prayer referenced the promises made to the Patriarchs.[179]

---

[176] e.g. Conflation occurs when "Old covenant" is taken to mean Old Testament. OC, biblically, is a reference to the Mosaic covenant, not the OT writings as a whole 2 Cor 3:7-16. Similarly, in Gal 4:21-31 it is the *Mosaic* covenant that is contrasted with the new order. In Hebrews, too, it is specifically the *Mosaic* covenant that is seen as *set aside* (7:18), *obsolete* (8:13), and *unlike the new* (8:9). In summary, obsolescence of the Mosaic covenant does not negate the Abrahamic, Davidic, and New covenants, the prophetic portions of Moses' writings or the other OT prophets - each of which demand Israel's ultimate restoration.
Other examples of failure to recognise distinctions: Israel vs church; events of 70AD vs events of Messiah's return; Mosaic law vs Messiah's law.

[177] Jn 1:45 See *Appendix: Messianic Prophecy*

[178] Luke 1:26-33. The terms used by Gabriel match directly the content of multiple OT prophecies.

[179] Luke 1:55

- Zechariah, too, spoke of Abraham's covenant, the prophets' promises and the future national deliverance from Israel's enemies.[180]

- The prophetess Anna was one of many longing for Jerusalem's redemption.[181]

- Having risen, it was to the Hebrew Scriptures that Messiah pointed, in verifying His identity.[182]

- *Everything* written about Messiah must be fulfilled, He assured his disciples.[183]

Matthew records Messiah's assurance that the apostles will one day judge Israel's twelve tribes, at the renewal of all things.[184]

Having been taught on the kingdom of God by the risen Messiah over a forty day period,[185] the apostles' only question recorded by Luke revealed

---

[180] Luke 1:69-74
[181] Luke 2:38
[182] Luke 24:25-27,32
[183] Luke 24:44,45
[184] Matt 19:28
[185] Acts 1:3

their firm expectation:
Is it now that you will restore Israel's kingdom?[186]

Following Pentecost, Peter, like those before him, referenced the restoration promised by the Old Testament prophets.[187] Paul too, later in his life, continued to proclaim and cling to the expectations of those same Hebrew prophets.[188]

Some insist that the New Testament is silent on Israel's land promises. If such a claim were true (and it is not), it would prove precisely nothing. Such an argument is as fallacious as suggesting that the Trinity is absent from Scripture simply because the term is not used.[189]

Israel's covenants, frequently mentioned and inferred in the New Testament, all have *known, spe-*

---

[186] Acts 1:6 Calvin's commentary hereon audaciously speaks of the apostles' *ignorance, foolishness, rudeness* and there being *as many errors in this question as words:*
https://biblehub.com/commentaries/calvin/acts/1.htm
But who could be better informed on this matter than those who had been personally tutored specifically on the kingdom of God by the resurrected Messiah over a 40 day period? (v3) The apostles' question concerned only timing - Messiah's response did not challenge their assumptions. (Messiah had not been slow to correct wrong assumptions held by the apostles e.g. Matt 16:23; 19:14; 20:22-28). The kingdom will be restored but Messiah would not tell the apostles when. He instead directed them to their interim mission, beginning in Jerusalem (Acts 1:8).

[187] Acts 3:19-21

[188] Acts 26:6,7; Rom 11:26,27;15:8

[189] In addition, even if the NT *were* silent, so what? The NT merely *assumes* many important OT matters and demonstrates no obligation to restate what has been plainly stated in the OT.

cific and *unambiguous* content in which the land is an essential component.[190] It is probably that very specificity and clarity that drives so many replacement theologians to declare that such promises have been *reinterpreted*.[191]

Messiah is said to have come to *confirm* Israel's promises, not bring about their negation.[192] We are told that God's gifts and calling are *irrevocable*, and that God's oath was added to make the unchanging nature of His purpose *very clear*, not to make it obscure or to change its meaning.[193]

Paul responds to the question, *Did God reject his people?* with an emphatic denial.[194] Far from reinterpreting the prophets, Peter teaches their words have been made *more certain*.[195]

---

[190] e.g. Luke 1:72; 22:20; Acts 3:25;7:8, Rom 9:4; 11:27; Gal 3:17; Eph 2:12 etc.

[191] See Chapter 5, *Replacement Theology* and Part II, *Reinterpretation*. Even the use of the term *reinterpretation* is an admission that the OT texts had a specific meaning, one that is now rejected.

[192] Rom 15:8 Again, it is the Mosaic covenant that Hebrews teaches has been made inoperative e.g. Heb 8:6-13. Israel's title deed to the land never depended on the Mosaic covenant - only their continuing occupation and enjoyment of the land in the OT period.

[193] Rom 11:29; Heb 6:17

[194] Rom 11:1

[195] 2 Pet 1:19

Just as in the Old Testament, Israel's regathering is the prerequisite and necessary implication of multiple New Testament prophecies.[196]

The Old Testament functions in the New Testament as a validating authority.[197] Indeed, Messiah validated His own identity in the Old Testament, and Paul and Peter firmly grounded their arguments in the same way.

Yet for replacement theologians the plain meaning of many Old Testament promises is simply to be rejected. Such behaviour is treated in the New Testament as unbelief.[198] Messiah, for example, portrays Abraham as saying that disregard for the writings of Moses and the Old Testament prophets leaves one impervious to evidence, even the miraculous.[199]

---

[196] e.g. Matt 24:14-31; Luke 1:33; 21:24; 2 Thes 2:4; Rev 11:1-13. De-Mar boldly declares, *"Nothing prophetic in the New Testament depends on Israel becoming a nation again."* One need only cite Messiah's own prediction of His return, explicitly predicated on recognition and welcome by the people of Jerusalem Mt 23:37-39.
It should be noted that Israel *never ceased to be a nation,* even though dispersed (Jer 31:36). Israel's dispersion was predicted in both testaments and has been fulfilled. Thus the necessary implication of Mt 23:37-39 is that at least part of the nation must be back in the land, Jerusalem in particular, prior to Messiah's return to earth.

[197] e.g. Jn 5:39,45-47; Acts 17:11; 2 Tim 3:16; 2 Pet 1:19-21

[198] Jn 5:45-47

[199] Luke 16:29-31 'If they do not listen to Moses and the Prophets, they will not be convinced even if someone rises from the dead.' (v31)

In the climax of the book of Romans, Paul demonstrates that the restoration of the Jewish people is assured, in accordance with the guarantees of the Old Testament covenants.[200] While the Jewish people have experienced *a hardening in part*, Paul assures his readers that when *the full number of Gentiles has come in*, the hardening will end.[201] He presses the point by declaring: *God's gifts and his call are irrevocable.*[202]

Having spoken in detail of the beauty of the divinely appointed interdependence of Jewish and non-Jewish redemption,[203] Paul erupts in praise of God's wisdom.[204]

The New Testament affirms the future restoration of Israel, as promised by the Hebrew prophets.

---

[200] Rom 11:26,27

[201] Rom 11:25. *Hardening in part* is a different proposition to the Jewish people being *temporarily set aside,* as is frequently taught even by those who affirm Israel's future restoration. Romans 11:1 rules out Israel's rejection, whether it be permanent or temporary. Noting the strength of the Greek used in 11:1 and its uses elsewhere in Romans, Sibley remarks that the notion of God rejecting Israel "was just as repugnant to Paul as the notion that God could be found to be unrighteous (Rom 3:5–6)" or "that we should sin in order that grace might increase" (referencing Rom 6:1-2). *Has The Church Put Israel On The Shelf?* JETS, 58/3, p577-578

[202] Rom 11:29

[203] Romans 11, especially vs11,12,15,25-32. God's covenant keeping faithfulness to Israel and the mystery of the relationship between Jewish and non-Jewish redemption forms the climax of the book of Romans.

[204] Rom 11:33-36

"And I will bless those
who bless you,

And the one who curses you
I will curse.

And in you all the families of
the earth will be blessed."

Genesis 12:3

7

RESPONSE AND RESPONSIBILITY

The non-Jewish world has never been an addendum or "Plan B" in God's covenantal programme of redemption. From Israel's inception, non-Jews are explicitly targeted for blessing via the nation that would come through Abraham. While God also promises to curse non-Jews in Genesis 12:3, in this context He is seen to do so only *reactively*.[205] When non-Jews hold Abraham and his nation in low regard (or worse), *then* God will curse.

That non-Jews would ultimately come in vast numbers to believe in the God of Israel, is made

---

[205] The two occurrences of *curse* in the English text translate two different Hebrew words. NET Bible renders the phrase *the one who treats you lightly I must curse*. (See also Num 24:9).

clear in the Old Testament.[206] Indeed, the prophets foresee a period of international peace inextricably linked with Israel's restoration and the nations being in right relationship with Israel.[207]

SALVATION HAS COME TO THE GENTILES TO MAKE ISRAEL ENVIOUS[208]

Among the purposes of non-Jews coming to believe in the Jewish Messiah in the current period, is that Jews might be provoked to jealousy. This is a concept with roots in the Old Testament. Moses made plain that God would be made angry and be provoked to jealousy by the unfaithfulness of His people Israel.[209] And that God would reciprocate by provoking Israel to jealousy.[210]

God's intention is that Jewish people today see in non-Jewish believers the knowledge and love of

---

[206] e.g. Isa 49:6; Mal 1:11. Unrevealed was that they would come without conversion to Judaism and be united with believing Jews in a new entity, the body of Messiah Eph 2:12-22; Rom 15:25,26. Gal 3:7 sees Gen 12:3b as the gospel announced in advance.

[207] e.g. Isa 2:1-4; 19:23-25; Zech 8:3-7;20-23

[208] Rom 11:11 NIV. Or NASB in full: *I say then, they did not stumble so as to fall, did they? May it never be! But by their transgression salvation has come to the Gentiles, to make them jealous.*

[209] Deut 32:16,21-25 The same word used of a husband's jealousy (Num 5:14) is taken by God as one of His names "...for the LORD, whose name is Jealous, is a jealous God..." Ex 34:14. Also Zech 8:2

[210] Deut 32:21b, Rom 10:19; 11:13,14 Jealousy can be defined as passionate desire for that which is rightfully one's own.

Israel's Messiah, and that they are made jealous thereby.[211]

Israel's failure has resulted in non-Jews experiencing great blessing.[212] That being so, how much greater blessing will the world enjoy when Israel is restored?[213] In a remarkable way, God has linked Jewish failure to non-Jewish redemption, and non-Jewish redemption to Israel's restoration.[214]

Non-Jewish believers are seen to be unnaturally grafted into an olive tree that belongs to the Jews.[215] Paul writes to Gentiles[216] (*the wild olive branches*), three times warning them concerning their attitude toward the Jews (*the natural branches*):

---

[211] Rom 11:11 Greek: parazēlóō, to stimulate alongside, i.e. excite to rivalry: provoke to emulation (jealousy). According to Fruchtenbaum: 'to come alongside someone and cause him to boil or seethe with jealousy'.

[212] Rom 11:12. Which was always a central purpose in God's election of Israel (Gen 12:3b).

[213] Rom 11:15 Paul here connects Israel's future acceptance of Messiah with resurrection.

[214] Rom 11:25-27,30-32

[215] Unnaturally grafted: Rom 11:17,24.
The text does not explicitly tell us what the olive tree represents. Eternal salvation, Israel, or the church are all problematic identifications, given the details provided in the context. "Provisional place of covenantal blessing" may be viable.
It is explicitly *their* [Israel's] *own olive tree* Rom 11:24

[216] Rom 11:13

"...do not boast over those branches..."
"...do not be arrogant, but be afraid..."
"...do not...be ignorant...
...so that you may not be conceited."[217]

The inference is that humility, knowledge and embrace of God's revelation concerning Israel, along with godly fear, will keep one from arrogance and conceit in this matter.[218]

These warnings alone suggest that Israel is not a peripheral matter within the biblical worldview. Biblical warnings of this kind have not been issued in regard to any other people group.

TO THE JEW FIRST

In the same epistle Paul declares the gospel to be *to the Jew first*.[219] Some scholars argue that the Greek construction demands that the gospel continues to be *to the Jew first*.[220] If the argument is sound, it has significant implications for the modern church. What is clear is that Paul himself, though specifically *the apostle to the Gentiles*, con-

---

[217] Rom 11:18,20,25

[218] *Boasting, arrogance, ignorance* and *conceit* have unfortunately been characteristics of much Christian theology. See Chapter 5, *Replacement Theology*

[219] Rom 1:16 Many commentators see 1:16 as the theme of Romans. However, it is often quoted in truncated form, without *to the Jew first and also to the Greek.*

[220] A useful summary of commentators' views: https://tinyurl.com/26waycrb

sistently acted in accordance with this principle.[221] Upon entering a new territory, apparently Paul always first addressed the local Jewish community.[222]

BIBLICAL EXAMPLES OF GENTILES DEDICATED TO THE JEWISH PEOPLE

Non-Jews with strong love for the Jewish people are conspicuous in the Scriptures and are singled out for special attention, in accordance with the principle of the Abrahamic Covenant.[223] Significantly, such love expressed itself in a very practical manner.

The Moabitess Ruth showed fierce loyalty to her Jewish mother-in-law, her people and her God.[224] She subsequently became a forbear of Messiah.[225]

The Centurion of Luke 7 was committed to the Jewish people and evidently had a strong relationship with the community.[226] He was highly commended by Messiah for his faith and his request for the healing of his servant was granted.[227]

---

[221] Acts 9:15; Gal 1:16; Rom 11:13

[222] e.g. Acts 13:5,46; 14:1; 17:10,17; 18:19; 19:8; 28:17

[223] Gen 12:3

[224] Rt 1:16-18

[225] Matt 1:5

[226] Luke 7:3-5

[227] Luke 7:9-10

Another Roman Centurion, Cornelius, was devout, showed kindness to, and earned a great reputation with the Jews.[228] Cornelius became one of the first non-Jews upon whom the Spirit was poured out.[229]

It is significant that in each case such dedication and kindness were shown to a biblically unrighteous nation.

EXAMPLES FROM THE MODERN PERIOD

In the modern period there are shining examples of Christian love toward the Jews. Notable international examples since the 1880s include:

Rev William Hechler (1845-1931). Hechler was one of several influential Bible believers spurred to action when pogroms broke out in Russia in 1881. With Lord Shaftesbury he established a committee to raise funds to assist Jews with resettlement. Proficient in ten major languages and two African dialects, and a student of Bible prophecy, Hechler was to become the tireless assistant and counsellor to Theodor Herzl, father of modern Zionism.

The need for a homeland and refuge had become obvious and Hechler used his significant diplo-

---

[228] Acts 10:1-2,22
[229] Acts 10:44,45

90

matic connections to maximum advantage in Herzl's cause.

Following Herzl's early death, Hechler repeatedly warned his Jewish friends there would be a massacre of Jews in Europe. His warnings were politely dismissed.[230]

William Blackstone (1841-1935) was a prominent American evangelist. Upon learning of the murder and rape of Russian Jews, Blackstone used his own funds to initiate a petition that would be signed by 413 influential Americans and presented to President Harrison.[231] It called for restoration of the Jews to their homeland. Blackstone "spoke out actively and aggressively against antisemitism, focusing in particular on the hatred spread by Henry Ford in his advocacy for the *Protocols of the Elders of Zion.*"[232] Blackstone was later called the "true" father of Zionism by a prominent Jewish leader.[233] It was Blackstone's view that:

---

[230] Wilkinson provides a detailed account of Hechler's activities in *Understanding Christian Zionism: Israel's Place in the Purposes of God*

[231] Later known as The Blackstone Memorial.

[232] The Protocols is a fabrication that continues to be promoted by antisemites: https://www.adl.org/resources/backgrounder/hoax-hate-protocols-learned-elders-zion
https://www.thefreelibrary.com/
Brandeis%2c+Wilson%2c+and+the+reverend+who+changed+history.-a0324589591

[233] Letter to Blackstone from Nathan Straus, after whom Netanya was named. According to Straus, Lois Brandeis agreed. Brandeis was a lawyer of the Supreme Court and leader and spokesperson of American Zionism.

...true Zionism is founded on the plan, purpose, and fiat of the everlasting and omnipotent God, as prophetically recorded in His Holy Word, the Bible.[234]

During World War II in Le Chambon, France, evangelical *Pastor Andre Trocme* led a community of mostly peasant villagers and farmers to rescue Jews fleeing the Nazis. Those Jews who found their way by rail to Le Chambon, Tence and other nearby villages, were typically met at the station and taken into hiding. A community of up to 5,000 risked their lives to rescue and shelter 3,500-5,000 Jews.[235]

Tragically though, the last seventeen centuries are mostly marked by Christian hostility - verbal, theological, and physical.

TWO MILLENNIA OF CHRISTIAN HOSTILITY

Jerusalem had been the geographical centre of the movement of followers of Jesus and remained so until the period of the second Jewish revolt, 132-135AD. Indeed, in the early years the movement was seen very much as a sect within Judaism. History records the names of the leaders of the Jerusalem-based movement prior to the second Jewish revolt and all are Jewish Christians.

---

[234] Rausch, *Zionism within early American Fundamentalism 1878-1918*, p268.
[235] https://holocaustfoundation.com/le-chambon

With Jews subsequently banned from Jerusalem, non-Jewish leaders became dominant. Many brought with them the platonic, gnostic and anti-Judaic ideas of their own native cultures. It was not long before a stance of open hostility became apparent.

A representative sample from the intervening centuries follows.

The First Council of Nicaea in 325 was significant in the development of a Christianity that chose to define itself in contradistinction to Judaism and its biblical roots. According to Boyarin:

[At Nicaea] Easter was severed once and for all within orthodox churches from its calendrical and thematic connections with Passover. In the end what was accomplished in Nicaea and Constantinople was the establishment of a Christianity that was completely separated from Judaism.[236]

The Council was convened by Emperor Constantine 272-337. His low regard for the Jews was plain in the letter he wrote to Christians who had not attended the Council:

We ought not, therefore, to have anything in common with the Jews... ...we desire, dearest brethren, to

[236] *The Jewish Gospels; The Story of the Jewish Christ,* loc 382, Kindle

separate ourselves from the detestable company of the Jews... ...they who, after the death of the Saviour, have no longer been led by reason but by wild violence... [237]

John Chrysostom 347-407, Church Father and Archbishop of Constantinople, wrote:

Jews are impure and impious, and their synagogue is a house of prostitution, a lair of beasts, a place of shame and ridicule, the domicile of the devil, as is the soul of the Jew... ...As a matter of fact, Jews worship the devil... [238]

Jerome, who died in 420, is most famous for the highly influential Latin Vulgate. He showed little warmth for the Jews. Of the Antioch synagogue he said:

---

[237] Constantine 306-337
https://sourcebooks.fordham.edu/source/const1-easter.asp

[238] Historian James Parkes comments on Chrysostom's eight *Homilies Against the Jews*: "There is no sneer too mean, no gibe too bitter for him to fling at the Jewish people. No text is too remote to be able to be twisted to their confusion, no argument is too casuistical, no blasphemy too startling for him to employ."
Donald Goldhagen, commenting on Chrysostom's influence, says: "The very definition of what it meant to be a Christian entailed a thoroughgoing and visceral hostility to Jews, just as it did to evil, and to the devil. It is no surprise that medieval Christians came to see Jews as agents of both."
Both quoted by Horner in *Future Israel*.

If you call it a brothel, a den of vice, the Devil's refuge, Satan's fortress, a place to deprave the soul... ...you are still saying less than it deserves.[239]

The period 500-1500 is described as one in which *the Jews, as a religious and a cultural minority, were often preyed upon by the Christian majority.*[240] While Jews have experienced expulsions throughout their history, in Christian Europe banishment began to occur with increasing frequency.[241]

The new millennium saw the blood libel become a recurrent theme. Jews were accused of kidnapping, torturing and murdering young Christian boys in order to use their blood in Passover bread. This became the pretext for many occasions of Christian violence against Jewish communities.[242]

That Jews should be condemned and shunned was a given in many European cultures. In 1233 Pope Gregory complained that German Jews were not living in *the state of complete misery to which they had been condemned by God.*[243]

---

[239] Wistrich, *The Longest Hatred,* p17

[240] https://tinyurl.com/2urb4j7w

[241] https://tinyurl.com/3nfk67dt

[242] According to Walter Lacquer, "there have been about 150 recorded cases of blood libel... ...that resulted in the arrest and killing of Jews..." *The Changing Face of Antisemitism: From Ancient Times to the Present Day*

[243] Hay, *Europe and the Jews: The Pressure of Christendom on the People of Israel for 1,900 Years*

The best known of the Reformers, German priest and theologian Martin Luther, 1483-1546, wrote:

(Jews are a) 'base, whoring people, that is, no people of God, and their boast of lineage, circumcision, and law must be accounted as filth... ...They are full of the devil's faeces... ...this insufferable devilish burden - the Jews.[244]

John Calvin, *as we have seen more moderate than Luther, nevertheless was rooted in the same essential Augustinian legacy. While not going out of his way to harass Jews, he was content to keep them out of Geneva and repeat traditional anti-Judaic statements.*[245]

Attempts to forcibly convert Jews were not uncommon. Following a 1648 refusal by Ukrainian Jews to convert to the Orthodox faith, Russian Cossacks instigated a slaughter:

Killing was accompanied by barbarous tortures; the victims were flayed alive, split asunder, clubbed to death, roasted on coals, or scalded with boiling water. Even infants at the breast were not spared.[246]

Moving to more recent times, as the antisemitic clouds darkened in Europe prior to World War II

---

[244] *The Jews and Their Lies*, 1543.
[245] Horner, *Future Israel*, p48
[246] https://tinyurl.com/2p86rdx2

...there is no evidence whatever of any authoritative statement being issued by the Evangelical Church calling for earnest consideration of the Jewish problem from a purely biblical standpoint...[247] Apparently many German churchmen were in fact thinking about the issue of the Jews in this period, but primarily in pursuit of the erasure of their influence. In 1934 eleven Protestant churches founded the *Institute for the Study and Elimination of Jewish Influence on German Church Life.*

Speaking of the later Nazi years, United States Holocaust Memorial Museum reports *...throughout this period there was virtually no public opposition to antisemitism or any readiness by church leaders to publicly oppose the regime on the issues of antisemitism and state-sanctioned violence against the Jews.*[248]

More broadly, Christians have tragically been implicated in many or most of history's anti-Jewish pogroms.[249]

In recent decades, an increasingly popular expression of Christian hostility has been Christian anti-

---

[247] Gutteridge referring to the Weimar period 1918-33 and quoted in *They Conspire Against Your People*, Colin Barnes, p29.

[248] https://encyclopedia.ushmm.org/content/en/article/the-german-churches-and-the-nazi-state
Dietrich Bonhoeffer and his colleagues were notable exceptions. https://tinyurl.com/47ztx7zr

[249] https://tinyurl.com/38t866bn

Zionism. Highly influential English evangelical theologian John Stott 1921-2011, said:[250]

I myself believe that Zionism, both political and Christian, is incompatible with biblical faith.[251]

Elsewhere he described Zionism as:
...anathema to Christian faith.[252]

We are not aware that Stott ever described as *anathema* any other indigenous people group's expression of national identity and self-determination.

CONCLUSION

Although it was God's express intention that the Gentile embrace of the Jewish Messiah would provoke Israel to jealousy, tragically, Christendom's conduct has more often been counterproductive to that divine purpose.[253]

---

[250] In 2005 Stott was listed among Time magazine's 100 most influential people in the world. That a high profile theologian could make such statements without widespread outcry from the Christian community is an indication of anti-Israel sentiment in much of Christendom.

[251] In Stott's endorsement of one of Stephen Sizer's books. https://tinyurl.com/2wmh2n64

[252] According to Wagner. https://en.wikipedia.org/wiki/Christian_Zionism

[253] Speaking of some of the religious Jews of his day, Paul wrote in Rom 2: *God's name is blasphemed among the Gentiles because of you.* Ironically, if Paul had lived many centuries later, he could have observed of Gentile Christendom: *Jesus' name is blasphemed among the Jews, because of you.*

Israel, the Jews, their land and city have long been a cause for controversy. Indeed, it is clear that Israel will, by design, increasingly operate as a cause of division in the Gentile world as history reaches its climax.[254]

In the here and now though, every believer and every Christian institution or community has a choice in regard to the Jews: to be an agent of *ignorance, arrogance* and *conceit* (to use Paul's terms), or, an agent of love, mercy and provocation to jealousy.

---

[254] Gen 12:3 infers that the non-Jewish world will divide into those who bless and those who curse Israel. That polarisation is made explicit by later biblical data, e.g. Num 24:9; Ezek 36:5; Joel 3:1-3; Matt 25:31-46.

Hear the word of the LORD,
O nations,
And declare in
the coastlands afar off,

And say,
"He who scattered Israel
will gather him

And keep him as a shepherd
keeps his flock."

Jeremiah 31:10

8

A MIXED RECORD AT THE ENDS OF THE EARTH

S ignificant examples of love and support for the Jewish people feature in New Zealand history. In recent decades, however, antagonism has become increasingly prevalent, both in the church and in society in general.

The 1800s saw increasing interest in the prophetic Scriptures in Britain largely as a consequence of the evangelical revival. The British missionary movement had a major role in New Zealand's establishment[255] and Britain long maintained a

---

[255] British missionaries were directly involved in facilitating the Treaty of Waitangi, considered the founding document of the nation.

strong cultural and political influence over the colony's society. By some accounts there were strong restorationist beliefs amongst British Anglicans of the time.[256] It is likely this influenced theological trends within New Zealand too. Restorationism was certainly evident within New Zealand's evangelical community in the first quarter of the twentieth century.

Groups with a restorationist, millennialist bent, saw the return of the Jews to Israel as a fulfilment of prophetic Scripture, the first stage in God's plan to ultimately inaugurate a thousand year reign of the Messiah from Jerusalem. One such institution was the New Zealand Bible Training Institute, a leading educational institutional for Evangelical Christians founded in 1922. The founder of the NZBTI, Rev. Joseph Kemp, articulated this view in an article published in the organisation's monthly magazine, The Reaper. Entitled 'The Jewish Tragedy', Kemp expounded an overview of Jewish history, past, present and future. He considered the present condition of the Jew as 'de-nationalised' and 'dispossessed', 'sad' and 'heart rending'. Yet he marvelled that they had retained their identity and were preserved as a people after centuries of persecution. This was, he considered, a miracle. Kemp argued that the welfare of the na-

---

[256] "The real advocates of Christian Zionism in Britain were primarily Anglican premillennialists. By the mid-19th century, about half of all Anglican clergy were evangelical premillennialists." Ice, The Case for Zionism, location 3993. Kindle.

tions was bound up in Israel's restoration. He taught that a restored Israel would bring 'universal peace and concord', and 'war and want' would be no more. In the decade leading up to the 1938 refugee crisis, many reports were published in The Reaper on progress in Palestine, antisemitism, Zionism, controversies, such as the fabricated 'Protocols of the Elders of Zion' and the British Israel 'heresy', as well teaching on Israel and prophecy from a biblical perspective. The words of the editor of The Reaper, J. Oswald Sanders, in 1938, represented a portion of the evangelical church that supported the restoration of the Jews. He wrote, 'Jerusalem is proving a burdensome stone to Britain, but we trust she will be true to the trust reposed in her, and keep Palestine for the Jews.[257]

In New Zealand society more generally, support for the restoration of the Jews to their homeland gathered momentum following the 1917 Balfour Declaration.[258] As an indication of the favour with which the cause was viewed, over two thousand attended the 1920 Wellington meeting of British Zionist emissary, Israel Cohen.[259]

---

[257] Sheree Trotter, doctoral thesis, University of Auckland, 2019.

[258] A statement by the British government expressing support for a "national home for the Jewish people."

[259] S. Trotter thesis "…credentials had been furnished by the Foreign Office and the Colonial Office, from the British Government to the Prime Minister…"

William Massey, New Zealand Prime Minister 1912-25, was a Zionist and was known to quote Scripture in support of Israel's restoration at public meetings. He was a strong advocate for the Jews in the post World War I European conferences.[260]

Peter Fraser's tenure as Prime Minister 1940-49 included the period of the Holocaust. Fraser too was a Zionist and often advocated on behalf of the Jews.[261] He led New Zealand in support of the 1947 United Nations vote for partition of Palestine, thus paving the way for the reestablishment of Israel.[262]

Despite New Zealand's role in Israel's rebirth, support for the Jewish state was to experience a sharp decline. This became particularly evident following the 1967 Six Day War, the 1973 Yom Kippur War and with the steady adoption by media and academia of the narratives of Palestinian Nationalism.

---

[260] Ibid.

[261] "However, Fraser was far more willing to support the return of the Jews to Palestine than the admission of refugees to New Zealand."
"Fraser believed strongly enough in the justice of the Zionist cause, that he was willing to challenge Britain. By 1947 Britain had given up hope of finding a solution to the Palestinian problem and signalled its intention to withdraw from Palestine, without making any provision for the maintenance of law and order. (Fraser) ...considered such an action to be neither responsible nor morally correct." Ibid.

[262] Ibid.

A jarring indicator of New Zealand's shift came late in 2016 with her sponsorship of the United Nations Security Council's deeply problematic Resolution 2334.[263] Co-sponsors were Venezuela and Senegal, along with Malaysia, considered to be one of the world's most antisemitic nations.[264]

New Zealand's voting record at the United Nations continues to display an anti-Israel bias and at the time of this writing New Zealand is a regular financial contributor to United Nations Relief and Works Agency, a body which funds school textbooks that are antisemitic and glorify terrorism against Jews.[265]

A number of New Zealand Members of Parliament have in recent years supported or associated with the antisemitic Boycott Divest Sanction

263 https://shalom.kiwi/2018/02/international-law-expert-new-zealand-made-a-terrible-mistake-at-the-un/
https://shalom.kiwi/2017/01/judenrein-jerusalem-new-zealands-shame/
264 https://www.timesofisrael.com/malaysia-gets-new-pm-with-history-of-controversial-comments-on-jews-israel/
265 https://israelinstitute.nz/2022/01/new-zealand-votes-to-fund-unprecedented-attack-on-israel/
https://israelinstitute.nz/2022/06/nz-silence-over-biassed-un-commission-of-inquiry/
https://israelinstitute.nz/2020/03/the-hypocrisy-of-new-zealands-donations-to-unrwa/
https://israelinstitute.nz/2022/09/new-zealand-announces-funding-for-glorification-of-terror-ahead-of-christchurch-call-to-action-leaders-summit/

movement.[266] Some have with impunity used the slogan *from the river to the sea, Palestine will be free,* a euphemistic call for the destruction of the Jewish state.[267]

In the area of Christian engagement with New Zealand's Jewish community, Rev Charles Chandler stands as model in the mid 1900s. As Anglican Dean of Hamilton, Chandler developed a close friendship with Rabbi Astor, Auckland's Rabbi for more than forty years. Chandler became a strong advocate for the Jews.[268] In 1971 Astor referred to Chandler as his 'oldest and closest friend' of over thirty years, praising his courage 'in championing the Jewish cause at times when we most needed friendship and understanding by the non-Jewish world.'[269]

However, Chandler's warmth was no indicator of Anglicanism's trajectory for the coming decades.

---

[266] https://israelinstitute.nz/2021/04/green-mp-accepts-petition-written-by-terror-affiliates-and-underpinned-by-flawed-report/
https://www.scoop.co.nz/stories/PO1905/S00291/nz-jewish-council-criticizes-christchurch-central-mp.htm
https://www.camera.org/article/backgrounder-the-intrinsic-anti-semitism-of-bds/

[267] https://shalom.kiwi/2021/05/nz-green-party-mp-tweets-call-for-israels-destruction/

[268] According to Astor, Chandler '…felt deeply the great injustice that had been done to the Jewish people through nearly 2,000 years of cruel hatred and persecution and he made it part of his life's work to break down this wall of misunderstanding and prejudice.' S. Trotter thesis.

[269] Ibid.

In the 1980s New Zealand Anglicans removed or substituted many of the occurrences of the terms *Zion* and *Israel* in their Psalter, apparently to create distance between biblical Israel and modern Israel. This was highly controversial and caused distress to many New Zealand Jews.[270] It was likened to actions of "the German church of the Nazi era" and was reported in international media.[271] A senior Australian academic described the move as "abhorrent."[272]

Elsewhere within the New Zealand church, matters took a similar turn.

What had formerly been known as *New Zealand Bible Training Institute* was renamed *Bible College of New Zealand* in 1972. By 2002 the strong support for restorationism had been replaced by antagonism toward the Jewish state and open disdain for the beliefs of the institution's founders.

---

[270] "There was outrage and hurt in the Jewish community…" https://liturgy.co.nz/psalter-revision

[271] "We regard the removal of the words Zion and Israel as profoundly anti-Jewish in effect… …the only precedent in this action appears to be in the German church of the Nazi era."
W. Ross, NZ Jewish Council, Jerusalem Post, Nov 29, 1989
Seven of eight Māori bishops spoke against the move as did D. Robinson, Archbishop of Sydney, Australia, who recognised the likeness to "the heresy of Marcion or the theological anti-Israel bias of some of the early church fathers…" Australian Jewish Times, 3 June 1988.

[272] "The idea of severing the Psalms from their origin is abhorrent." Prof Edwin Judge, Macquarie University. AJT, 22 April 1988. Judge had been a member of the Australian Liturgical Commission.

A 2002 issue of Bible College of New Zealand's *Reality* magazine was entitled *The Question of Israel.*[273] It included replacement theology, anti-Zionism, and blatant and ahistorical propaganda, for example:

"...a non-violent revolt - the first intifada...",[274] *"Israeli imperialism..."*,[275] and *"...Jesus Christ, who was himself a Palestinian under occupation..."*[276]

Bible College of New Zealand in 2008 changed its name to *Laidlaw College*, in memory of Robert Laidlaw 1885-1971. Laidlaw was one of *New Zealand Bible Training Institute's* founders and was, ironically, a supporter of the Jews.

The Gospel and the Land of Promise was published in 2009, featuring chapters mostly by authors from Laidlaw College[277] and Carey Baptist College. Largely an anti-Zionist, supersessionist work, it included ahistorical claims, anachronisms and both logical and theological fallacies.[278] It served to further undermine traditional Christian support for Israel.

---

[273] *Reality*, June-July 2002
[274] p14. There were heavy casualties in the first intifada. https://www.jewishvirtuallibrary.org/first-intifada
[275] p14. https://www.emmausroad.org.nz/whos-colonising-whom/
[276] p17.
[277] It is not here implied that all Laidlaw teachers necessarily hold problematic views of Israel.
[278] Several examples are given in Part II, *Turning The Text On Its Head*

World Vision New Zealand, ostensibly a Christian agency, in 2011 sponsored the showing of the anti-Israel film *With God On Our Side*,[279] described as propaganda by commentators.[280] It included at least one fabricated quote. Internationally, World Vision has a long and well documented history of anti-Israelism and has been shown to have "ties to terrorism".[281]

In 2012 Laidlaw College in cooperation with Tear Fund NZ hosted UK Anglican Priest Rev Dr Stephen Sizer, notorious as perhaps the leading Christian anti-Zionist of the period. Sizer has long been accused of antisemitism and association with Holocaust deniers and terrorists. He was ultimately formally charged and found guilty of anti-

---

[279] Report on file by Kirsty Walker, who attended a showing.

[280] https://tinyurl.com/53j4f528

[281] https://tinyurl.com/yck7srh5
World Vision's Gaza manager was indicted in 2016 and convicted in 2022 for assisting terrorist entity Hamas:
https://www.jpost.com/israel-news/article-709457
"In 2019, the U.S. Senate Finance Committee began investigating World Vision because of allegations that the group had intentionally partnered with the Islamic Relief Agency (ISRA), which is listed by the Office of Foreign Assets Control (OFAC) as a sanctioned entity because of its ties to terrorist groups. The committee's report, issued in December 2020, concluded that monetary contributions made to World Vision ended up aiding terrorist activities." https://www.nationalreview.com/corner/world-visions-troubling-ties-to-terrorism/
"Most of World Vision's terror-finance scandals involve funding violent, anti-Israel groups."
https://www.meforum.org/64207/world-vision-friend-of-terrorists

semitic acts by a disciplinary tribunal of his own UK Anglican Church.[282]

That Rev Dr Sizer's appearance at Laidlaw College was no anomaly is evidenced by the fact that speakers holding problematic views in common with Sizer were hosted by the institution in the years prior.[283]

Also in 2012, a senior theology lecturer at Laidlaw College publicly expressed his wish to see Israel isolated by the West.[284] In the same period Tear Fund New Zealand leaders made various statements misrepresenting the Israeli/Palestinian conflict and functioned as soft apologists for Palestinian terror.[285]

As of 2020 Laidlaw teaching materials continued to feature replacement theology and anti-Zionism.

---

[282] https://news.sky.com/story/vicar-who-shared-controversial-9-11-article-engaged-in-antisemitic-activity-tribunal-finds-12799583
https://tinyurl.com/4kk9xvsc
https://tinyurl.com/45755pab
https://www.bbc.com/news/uk-64460767

[283] Alex Awad, Bethlehem Bible College, and Peter Walker, Oxford.

[284] "…When will the West wake up and begin to isolate Israel until they comply with international law." P. Church, May 2012

[285] https://www.evangelicalzionism.com/tear-fund-nz-2012
Tear Fund NZ's Frank Ritchie, in a video discussion with Rev Dr Stephen Sizer, inferred moral equivalence between IDF actions and those of Palestinian terrorists, saying, among other things, "…I would rather do away with the term terrorism…"

Turning back to the 1900s, the Holocaust impacted New Zealand's Jewish community very directly with many having relatives trapped in Europe. Large numbers of Jews sought refuge in New Zealand both prior to and during the Holocaust and about 1,100 were admitted. Thousands more were denied entry.[286]

Six million Jews were murdered in the Holocaust, and 1946 saw many of the survivors in need as refugees in Europe. Upon learning of their desperate plight, several Christian Nga Puhi kaumatua[287] travelled by train to Wellington to offer the New Zealand government 1200 acres on which to house Jewish refugees. They were told "go back to your hovels." The land was later confiscated by the government.[288]

Following World War II, many Nazis fled to western nations to avoid prosecution for their crimes. According to Nazi Hunter Dr Efraim Zuroff:

New Zealand was the only Anglo-Saxon country, (out of Great Britain, United States, Canada and Australia - South Africa was not open to immigration at that time), that chose not to take legal action

---

286 Ann Beaglehole, *A Small Price to Pay*
287 Elders of NZ's indigenous people, the Māori.
288 According to Nga Puhi Kaumatua Pat Ruka, unpublished film shot 2018.

after a governmental enquiry into the presence of Nazis in New Zealand.[289]

In the 1980s New Zealand's ignominy with regard to the Holocaust crossed a significant boundary in the academic arena. New Zealand gained the distinction of being the only western nation in which an MA degree has been awarded for a work of Holocaust denial or revisionism.[290] Christchurch's University of Canterbury awarded an MA to Joel Hayward for a work that concluded "the Nazis did not... ...have extermination policies as such". Esteemed historian Professor Emeritus Sir Richard Evans[291] described the thesis in question as "a thoroughly tendentious, biased and dishonest piece of work".

The above survey, though far from complete, illustrates the drift from New Zealand's widespread stance of favour toward the Jewish people (and, more recently, toward the Jewish state), to one of

---

[289] https://tinyurl.com/yjf578c9
Dr Efraim Zuroff, "The Last Nazi Hunter", is an historian and is director of the Jerusalem office of the Simon Wiesenthal Center.

[290] https://shalom.kiwi/2017/12/canterbury-universitys-academic-credibility-found-wanting/
https://shalom.kiwi/2017/04/kiwi-link-denial-canterbury-tales/
https://shalom.kiwi/2017/10/denial-film-shows-truth-matters-new-zealand-universities-disagree/

[291] Evans' courtroom encounter with notorious Holocaust denier David Irving is portrayed in the popular film *Denial*.
https://holocaustfoundation.com/denial

increasing political, academic and theological hostility.

*For the LORD has
a day of vengeance,*

*A year of recompense for
the controversy of Zion.*

Isaiah 34:8

9

ANTISEMITISM AND ITS UNSEEN CAUSE[292]

To the atheist, antisemitism[293] seems largely irrational and inexplicable. For the biblically minded believer, however, antisemitism is entirely rational and serves as a strong validation of the biblical worldview.

---

[292] Portions of this chapter have been adapted from the author's: *Artist Statement* for the *Auschwitz. Now.* Exhibition. https://holocaustfoundation.com/artist-statement
Yom HaShoah Speech at Auckland Hebrew Congregation, 2022. https://holocaustfoundation.com/blog/2022/5/6/what-really-changed-in-1945-yom-hashoah-speech

[293] Jew hatred. *Antisemitism* is a relatively modern term, probably coined by German journalist Wilhelm Marr in 1879. The hatred it denotes, however, is thousands of years old and has been dubbed "The Oldest Hatred".

Persecution has been an unrelenting theme in Jewish history.[294] Indeed, three of Judaism's major feasts commemorate victory in the face of attempts to destroy the Jewish people.[295] Today there are more than fifteen million Jews worldwide, but still fewer than in the period prior to the Holocaust. If there had never been persecution of the Jews, their population today would be very much greater.

Antisemitism has been the subject of a vast mass of scholarly research. However, there is yet to be a universally accepted naturalistic theory as to why a people group so numerically insignificant has been the subject of millennia of hatred.[296]

Although Jews constitute just 2% of USA's population they are more often the targets of religious hate crimes than any other group, by a large margin.[297] In many western cities today, Jews avoid

---

[294] https://www.simpletoremember.com/articles/a/historyjewish-persecution/

[295] Pesach (Passover) celebrating deliverance from Egypt (and from the genocide of Ex 1); Purim (Lots), celebrating the thwarting of Haman's planned genocide; Hanukkah (Lights) commemorating the rededication of the temple and victory over Antiochus Epiphanes' forced assimilation of Jews.

[296] According to Jewish commentator Denis Prager. *Why The Jews?*, Prager and Telushkin
Jews make up approximately 0.2% of the world population.

[297] e.g. https://ucr.fbi.gov/hate-crime/2019/topic-pages/tables/table-1.xls

wearing visible signs of their identity for fear of physical attack.[298]

Antisemitism manifests in many forms. This chapter will limit itself to a brief description of the Holocaust, rhetorical questions concerning its aftermath, and a biblical explanation of antisemitism. A separate appendix is included in this book, providing a survey of some of the major expressions and sources of antisemitism.

THE HOLOCAUST

There have been genocides of various people groups and yet the Nazi sponsored attempt to eradicate the Jews in the years to 1945 stands as unique. The intention was to kill every Jewish man, woman and child, as an end in itself.[299] Large numbers of Roma and Sinti, homosexuals, and other groups were murdered.[300] But it was Jews who were most intensively targeted. The killing of Jews had no pragmatic justification.[301]

---

[298] https://www.timesofisrael.com/poll-nearly-half-of-uk-jews-avoid-visible-signs-of-judaism-due-to-anti-semitism/ https://www.bbc.com/news/world-europe-43884075

[299] The killing would not have been limited to Europe. It was the wish of Haj Amin al-Husseini that Jews would likewise be annihilated in the Middle East: https://www.jewishvirtuallibrary.org/the-mufti-and-the-f-uuml-hrer

[300] The oft-quoted figure of 5 million non-Jewish victims is incorrect: https://tinyurl.com/5b3ptsct

[301] Such as the acquisition of territory.

Europe's Jewish population in the 1930's numbered some nine million. Poland was at that time home to the world's largest Jewish community. It had been so for centuries. By the time World War II ended, six million European Jews had been murdered and ninety per cent of Polish Jews were dead. Many had been reduced to ashes by facilities purpose built by Hitler's regime.[302]

The systematic murder of Jews on an industrial scale was no historical anomaly. Rather, it was merely the worst manifestation of a hatred that for hundreds of years had simmered and frequently boiled over. Ancient hatred, German efficiency and technology converged with theological, Darwinian and other ideologies, to destroy a people. Europe of the time was considered Christian and Germany the pinnacle of culture and education. And yet it spawned such evil.

Industrialised killing on such a scale was only possible because of the cooperation of ordinary Europeans - whether it be active or passive. Many of the Jews' former neighbours became eager accomplices in their murder. Few resisted. Those who showed compassion toward the Jews often did so at great personal risk. Amongst the most disturbing of many disturbing facts that emerge from

---

[302] Recent research suggests 44,000 Nazi camps for incarceration, slave labour and killing: https://tinyurl.com/2ctaujp4

survivor accounts, is that examples of love and courage toward the Jews were so few.[303]

Assimilation and a renunciation of their "chosen-ness" proved to be an ineffective strategy for many Jews seeking relief from antisemitism. German Jews in the 1930s and 1940s often saw themselves more as Germans than as Jews and fully embraced the culture. Many such assimilated Jews perished in Auschwitz' gas chambers.

Antisemitism's force was seen in Hitler's compulsion in the closing stages of the war to prioritize the murder of Jews over the supply of resources to the front lines.

WHAT REALLY CHANGED IN 1945?

The allies prevailed in 1945 and the death camps were liberated. But in regard to the root causes of the Holocaust, what really changed?

- Did ordinary Europeans repudiate the Jew hatred that for centuries had manifested in economic, social and religious discrimination?

- Were the masses of willing accomplices brought to account, or at least filled with remorse?

---

[303] https://holocaustfoundation.com/stories

- Did the philosophers who influence society from above, abandon their intolerance of Jewish distinction and particularity?

- Did theologians reject the toxic and incoherent supersessionism that for centuries had driven Christian persecution of Jews?

- Was there a change of heart in the Muslim leaders so keen to see Hitler's policies implemented in their own lands?

- Were the western political and military leaders who knew what was happening to European Jews and yet chose to do little or nothing - were they brought to account?

- Of the many nations that chose to close their doors to Jews fleeing certain calamity, how many were willing to acknowledge their moral failure?

- How many nations cooperated with subsequent attempts to bring Nazis to justice?

The implications of these seldom asked questions are disturbing and increasingly relevant.

A Biblical Explanation

The Scriptures provide only brief glimpses of the spiritual battlefield[304] and yet its influence on the actions of men and nations is profound.[305] Paul sees believers as participants in a spiritual war involving the thought life, ideas and spiritual entities.[306] While such entities operate in the unseen realm, their influence outworks in the material world, in human history.

From the time of the promise to create a unique nation from Abram, there have been ongoing attempts to disrupt God's programme and destroy His people.[307]

Old Testament prophecy positioned the Jews as central and essential to Messiah's first coming.[308] Prophecy from both testaments sees the Jews as

---

[304] e.g. Gen 3:1-6,15; Deut 32:8,9ESV; 1 Chr 14:15; Dan 10:12,13,20;12:1; Acts 5:3; 1Pet 5:8; Jude 9; Rev 12:4-9,13-17

[305] Eph 2:2; 1 Jn 5:19

[306] 2 Cor 10:3-5; Eph 6:12

[307] e.g. Gen 12:10-20; 20:1-1 7; Ex 1:15-22 (had this policy continued, it would have been the end of the Jewish nation); Est 3:8-14. In the last two millennia: innumerable pogroms and expulsions; the Holocaust; ongoing genocidal Arab hostility against Israel since 1948 (and more recently Persian hostility also).

[308] e.g. Gen 49:10; Num 24:17; Deut 18:15; Isa 9:6;11:1; Zech 9:9; Mic 5:2; (See also Matt 2:1-2; Rom 9:5)

equally essential to His return[309] and the establishment of His kingdom.[310] That being so, the adversary was, and is, supremely motivated to destroy the Jewish people, to promulgate Jew hatred and to cultivate denial of Jewish connection to the land and to Jerusalem.

It is not coincidental that antagonism toward Israel and Jewish Jerusalem, and the despair of the Jewish people, reach their climax in the events immediately preceding Messiah's promised return to the earth.[311] Although Jewish history has been tragically littered with calamitous events, Moses, the Hebrew prophets and Messiah Himself all spoke of the uniqueness of this future period of distress.[312] It will end with Israel's warrior King responding to penitent Israel's plea, directly intervening to crush Israel's enemies.[313]

---

[309] Num 24:17-19; Isa 59:20; Jer 23:5-7; Joel 3:1-3; Zech 12:10-13:2;14:2-4; Matt 23:37-39; Acts 3:19-21. Significantly, a number of OT prophecies present first and second coming data in the same immediate context e.g. Isa 9:6,7; 61:1-7; Zech 9:9,10; Mic 5:2-5. To interpret first coming prophecy at face value and yet spiritualize second coming data in the same context as though it is fulfilled in the church is inconsistent and untenable. See Chapter 5, *Replacement Theology*.

[310] e.g. Gen 49:10b; Ps 102:13-17; Isa 2:1-5; 4:3-6; 9:7; Jer 31:7-14; Mic 4:2; Zech 8:2-23; 14:9-10,16-21; Matt 19:28; Luke 1:32-33; Acts 1:3,6-8

[311] Zech 12:1-3

[312] Deut 32:36-43; Dan 12:1,7; Jer 30:7; Matt 24:21

[313] Zech 12:9,10; 14:2-3; Ps 110:6

When the church disregards or even opposes the Jewish people, or simply ignores the ample biblical data concerning "the controversy of Zion",[314] debilitating confusion is created and the church fails to align with God's purposes.

Understood biblically, antisemitism serves as a remarkable (yet deeply tragic) confirmation of the Scriptures' veracity and the fact that we operate in a spiritual war zone. Israel's land, city, people and King will one day be the centre of non-Jewish attention and affection.[315] Therefore, it should not surprise us if in the interim they become a cause of great controversy.

As antisemitism continues to surge it will be increasingly important for believers to view this phenomenon through a biblical lens and to resolve to think and respond accordingly.[316]

---

[314] Isa 34:8; 61:2; 63:4; Ezek 35:5-9; 36:5-7; Rev 12:13

[315] e.g. Isa 2:1-3; 14:1,2; 49:22-23; 60:3; Zech 8:20-23; 14:16; Zep 3:19,20

[316] Increase in antisemitism: https://tinyurl.com/84uvcy9a https://tinyurl.com/4tftjwmt https://tinyurl.com/yfkytj83

Oh, the depth of the riches
of the wisdom
and knowledge of God!
How unsearchable his judgments,
and his paths beyond tracing out!
Who has known
the mind of the Lord?
Or who has been his counsellor?
Who has ever given to God,
that God should repay him?
For from him and through him
and to him are all things.
To him be the glory forever!
Amen.

Romans 11:33-36

10

CONCLUSION

This book leaves much unsaid. It has little to say on the details of eschatology, including the sequence of predicted events and how the current situation in the Middle East may align with biblical prophecy. Likewise, the full theological implications of a sound view of Israel (or conversely, of replacement theology) remain unaddressed.

In the geopolitic sphere there exist questions relating to the legality of modern Israel's founding, her conduct in mitigating threats and attacks from her genocidal enemies, and of course the oft-heard accusations of colonialism, apartheid, occupation and sometimes even genocide. The indigenous claims of the Jewish people and of the Arabs are addressed only briefly. There is also the crucial matter of who is really responsible for the sad plight of many Palestinians.

A comprehensive treatment of the above is a matter for other volumes and other writers. The present writer's intention has been to provide an outline of relevant foundational matters from a perspective that holds Scripture to be authoritative.

A biblical worldview is one that does more than pay lip service to biblical authority. It is one that ultimately develops a coherent position, adequately accounting for all the biblical data without resorting to the kinds of theological evasion outlined in Part II.

It has been argued that the very veracity of the canon of Scripture is at stake in consideration of the issue of Israel's restoration. No biblical theme is granted more prominence and none is articulated in more emphatic language. If, as the supersessionists claim, the promises of Israel's restoration are annulled, reinterpreted, or otherwise transformed so that they no longer mean what they meant to their human authors and first readers, then no biblical statement can be relied upon.

However, if the position presented in this book is sound, then it is appropriate to ask, *So what? What now?*

A believer's appropriate response to this matter can be expressed by the verbs *think, pray, speak, act.* It is our thoughts on a matter that determine our words and subsequent actions. Study of the biblical text, combined with humility, prayer and the application of God-given reason should, over time, result in a sound view of a subject. If the Scriptures are truly a presentation of what God has chosen to reveal on a matter, then it is our privilege to seek to understand that information and then to align our thoughts, prayers, speech and actions accordingly.[317]

Of course, even when there is unity of conviction among believers, actions taken by various individuals will likely differ markedly. After all, each believer has a unique set of opportunities and circumstances, and each is gifted differently.[318] Individuals may express their commitment to God's revealed intentions for Israel through prayer, worship, evangelism, advocacy, humanitarian service, fighting antisemitism and replacement theology, giving, and more.

For Christian communities and congregations, there are implications, too. If it is true that the leaders of a congregation are responsible to faithfully teach the content of Scripture, then it is reasonable to expect that the issue of Israel will be taught and taught properly. Over a given period it is appropriate that Israel's place in the biblical worldview is given a prominence comparable to its prominence in Scripture.

---

[317] Deut 29:29; Prov 25:2
[318] Rom 12:4-8; 1 Cor 12:4-11

Such an approach would be equally appropriate when asking how the matter of Israel should impact corporate prayer, worship, missions, giving and humanitarian service.

This book has argued that most of Christendom has distorted or ignored much of the vast body of biblical data on Israel. Despite the schemes of men, however, the Bible continues to speak plainly of Israel's centrality in the biblical worldview and of her ultimate restoration. The Jewish people, for centuries scattered throughout the nations, have been partially regathered and their presence as an indigenous people in their ancestral land and city has become a cause of great controversy. Realities on the ground may transform this issue from one that many view as a mere theological curiosity to one that demands urgent attention. It is quite possible that world events will in the coming years require of believers much more than mere intellectual assent.

Finally: though the matter of Israel has always been controversial (just as God intended), for biblically-minded believers it is also a source of great wonder and joy. In a remarkable and worship-worthy way, God's dealings with Israel vividly demonstrate in time and space, His grace, His wisdom and His faithfulness.

PART II

TURNING THE TEXT ON ITS HEAD

HOW REPLACEMENT THEOLOGY ARGUES ITS CASE

The purpose of this section is to expand upon Chapter 5's taxonomy of replacement theology's presuppositions and methods, and to provide examples from the writings of its proponents.

I t is hoped that the reader by now recognises that the biblical promises of Israel's ultimate restoration are numerous and that most are very clear. Indeed, many replacement theologians, in moments of candour, acknowledge that they too recognise that Israel's restoration is predicted in Scripture.

Now we must frankly admit that a literal interpretation of the Old Testament prophecies gives us just such a picture of an earthly reign of the Messiah as the premillennialist pictures.[319]

Floyd Hamilton here acknowledges that the Old Testament, taken at face value, does indeed teach Israel's restoration.

Highly respected theologian, Loraine Boettner stated:

It is generally agreed that if the prophecies are taken literally, they do foretell a restoration of the nation of Israel in the land of Palestine with the Jews having a prominent place in that kingdom and ruling over the other nations.[320]

GK Beale makes a similar acknowledgement:

Perhaps one of the most striking features of Jesus' kingdom is that it appears not to be the kind of kingdom prophesied in the OT and expected by Judaism.[321]

---

[319] Floyd Hamilton, *The Basis of the Millennial Faith,* Grand Rapids, 1942, p. 38

[320] Loraine Boettner, "Postmillennialism," ed. Robert G. Clouse, *The Meaning of the Millennium: Four Views,* Downers Grove, 1977, p. 95. Quoted by Richard Mayhue, '*New Covenant Theology and Futuristic Premillennialism',* The Master's Journal, 18/1 (Fall 2007) p.223. https://www.tms.edu/m/tmsj18j.pdf

[321] https://tinyurl.com/3rrvvry8

Beale here admits that the Old Testament's prophetic description does not match the kingdom that he believes now exists in fulfillment of Old Testament predictions.

Despite the above admissions, replacement theologians are adamant that the position taken in this book is mistaken, and that Israel will *not* be nationally restored in the manner described in the Old Testament or, as has been argued in Chapter 6, as both assumed and affirmed in the New Testament.

How then do replacement theologians argue their case?

What follows is a brief survey of some of the key assumptions, concepts and strategies of replacement theology. Many of the listed ideas are closely related and some of the strategies are employed simultaneously. Examples from the writings of supersessionists are provided.

I. Reinterpretation

Key terms and concepts are said to be reinterpreted and redefined by New Testament writers. Once accepted as a legitimate approach, reinterpretation can be used to overturn any Old Testament statement or concept.

P rofessor NT Wright is a gifted and highly influential scholar with whom many evangelicals are enamoured.[322] It is clear from Wright's writings that he believes the New Testament reinterprets the Old Testament:

Jesus explicitly hooked his own announcement into the ancient prophecies... ...and he radically reinterpreted its meaning...[323]

Jesus spent his whole ministry redefining what the kingdom meant. He refused to give up the symbolic language of the kingdom, but filled it with such new content that, as we have seen, he powerfully subverted Jewish expectations.[324]

---

[322] Presently a senior research fellow at Wycliffe Hall at the University of Oxford.

[323] https://tinyurl.com/4up6w6hr

[324] *Jesus and the Victory of God*, p249.

Gary Burge holds a similar view:[325]

For as we shall see (and as commentators regularly show) while the land itself had a concrete application for most in Judaism, Jesus and his followers reinterpreted the promises that came to those in his kingdom.[326]

Peter Walker states:[327]

...Jesus and the New Testament writers have given a definitive reinterpretation of this restoration theme—a reinterpretation that is authoritative and thus disallows us from seeking fulfillment of these promises in ways that seem to undermine the reality of the fulfillment offered by Jesus.[328]

According to Bruce Waltke:

...in the New Testament... ...the Old Testament's use of the term land with reference to Canaan is resignified to encompass the whole earth...[329]

Thus it is claimed the New Testament *reinterprets, resignifies* or *redefines* various terms and concepts

---

[325] Formerly Professor of New Testament Emeritus, Wheaton College
[326] *Jesus and the Land*, p35
[327] Wycliffe Hall, University of Oxford
[328] GLP, p7 Kindle.
[329] *A Genesis Commentary*, p65, ePub edition.
Waltke here appeals to Rom 4:13. See *II. Proof Texting*.

so that the promises and prophecies of the Old Testament no longer mean what they meant to the writers and first readers of the Old Testament.

It is surprising and somewhat disturbing that those professing a high view of Scripture readily accept such a notion. We need not read more than a few pages of Scripture to encounter the first recorded *reinterpretation* of God's words to man.[330] God's hostility to such behaviour was extreme and the consequences for man have been profound.[331]

God is creator and therefore both the source of information and the one who devised the means of its communication.[332] It ought to be self evident that He is therefore the consummate communicator, entirely able to communicate so as to be satisfactorily understood.

Throughout Scripture we encounter God communicating to man (usually through the prophets). It becomes unavoidably obvious that He holds man responsible for that which He has communicated. Especially where commands are involved, there are consequences for disregard of

---

[330] Gen 2:16,17; 3:1-4

[331] We can not comprehend the severity of the consequences of the fall, having never experienced an unfallen world. Gen 3:11-19

[332] In this case, the spoken and written word.

His words.[333] Of course not all that God has chosen to communicate involves commandments and prohibitions. Frequently it is the unfolding of future events that occupies the biblical writer.[334]

Among the reasons God reveals the future are the following:

- to show that He is God;[335]

- to glorify Messiah;[336]

- to provide warning;[337]

- to enable recognition and understanding of periods, events and persons;[338]

- to comfort and encourage;[339]

- to involve His servants in the execution of His plans and to enable their alignment with His priorities and purposes.[340]

---

[333] Old Testament Israel's history is a catalogue of failure to heed that which God had commanded, and the consequences thereof.

[334] Scripture's content is multifaceted.
It has been suggested that 17.5% of Scripture was predictive at the time it was written. Payne, p681. https://tinyurl.com/bdet47je

[335] Prophecy demonstrates His omniscience and omnipotence. Isa 44:7; 48:3

[336] Rev 19:10

[337] e.g. Gen 2:17; Matt 24:15-17; Luke 21:20-24

[338] e.g. Gen 15:16; Dan 9:27; and most notably, to enable recognition of the Messiah. See *Appendix: Messianic Prophecy*

[339] e.g. Isa 54:1-8; Dan 12:9,10; Matt 19:28-30

[340] e.g. Isa 62:6,7; Amos 3:7; Luke 1:30-33

Several of these categories have particular relevance in regard to the restoration of Israel and believers today. God *has* made plain that He will ultimately restore Israel and that knowledge enables believers to think, pray, speak and act appropriately in the light of current and future events.

According to Price, *this time of future blessing is mentioned and expanded upon by every prophetic book in the Old Testament except Jonah.*[341] Given the sheer volume of biblical data concerning the restoration of Israel, we must assume it is very important for believers to understand and affirm this matter.[342]

It is readily admitted that not all Scripture is equally clear.[343] But in the case of the many passages that plainly teach Israel's restoration, replacementists Hamilton, Boettner and Beale have clearly demonstrated that *even they have understood* what those texts are communicating.[344] The passages are clear. And yet replacementists insist the

---

[341] *What Should We Think About Israel?* Price (Ed.), loc 601, Kindle

[342] Elsewhere the author has made the claim that no biblical theme is given greater prominence than Israel and God's intention to restore His people to their land and to Himself. https://www.evangelicalzionism.com/
Affirmation of Israel's ultimate restoration does *not* equate to support for everything modern Israel does. See Chapter 3, *Thinking Biblically About Israel*

[343] Where texts may seem unclear, an appropriate approach is to begin with texts that *are* clear and allow those to assist in understanding less clear passages.

[344] Quoted in the opening paragraphs of this section.

obvious meanings have been overturned or reinterpreted by the New Testament.

If these replacementists are correct, and texts that once meant one thing now mean something unrecognisably different (the former meaning being false, the latter meaning being true), is it possible to avoid the conclusion that God was deceiving the Old Testament prophets, and their first listeners and readers?

No. It is not.

As demonstrated in Chapter 6, Messiah held His hearers responsible for that which had been revealed in the Old Testament. He went so far as to portray Abraham as saying that disregard for the writings of Moses and the Old Testament prophets leaves one impervious to evidence, even the miraculous.[345] If Old Testament meaning can be, and has been changed, then Messiah's position becomes untenable and incoherent, and certainly unjust.[346]

---

[345] Luke 16:29-31 'If they do not listen to Moses and the Prophets, they will not be convinced even if someone rises from the dead.' (v31)

[346] One can not be held responsible to believe a statement, the meaning of which has since changed.
Lest it be objected that Messiah's credentials and prediction of Israel's restoration are entirely different matters (the latter being reinterpreted), observe that in some cases Messiah's first and second coming *and* Israel's restoration are all woven together in the same context e.g. Num 24:17-18; Isa 9:6-7; Mic 5:2-4.

"Denotative Distance"

With verbal and written communication we may speak of the sender and the receiver. The message is the information intended to make the journey from the mind of the sender to the mind of the receiver. Assuming competence and virtue on the part of both sender and receiver, communication will be successful. Any difference between the meaning intended by the sender and the meaning taken by the receiver indicates a deficiency of competence or virtue in one or both parties.

In the case of God's communication to man in Genesis 2, we may assume supreme competence and virtue on God's part. We may also assume adequate competence on the part of the man and woman. Interference and lack of human virtue meant that God's message was distorted.[347] And the results were catastrophic.[348]

The difference between God's message in Genesis 2 and its distortion in Genesis 3 could be called "denotative distance."

What have the previous few paragraphs to do with replacement theology?

---

[347] Gen 3:1-4
[348] Gen 3:14-24

The point is this: *the distance between God's words in Genesis 2 and how they were distorted in Genesis 3, is in many cases less than the distance between God's words concerning Israel's restoration and replacement theology's distortion thereof.*

Of course there is much more to biblical interpretation and sound hermeneutics than this, but *there is not less than this.* Words mean things.[349]

God *can* communicate and has done so concerning Israel's restoration. No statement in Scripture is more emphatic than those concerning His determination to restore the Jewish people to Himself and to their land.[350] It is not a trivial matter to ignore, deny, obfuscate, or reinterpret what God has made comprehensible.

It is not difficult to demonstrate that Abraham, Noah, and Isaiah understood the prophecies they were given, directly in accordance with the words and phrases used. It is true that Old Testament prophets did not fully understand the entire substance of their own writings.[351] But Abraham understood the land promise truly referred to a spe-

---

[349] See, for example: *Evangelical Hermeneutics: The New Versus the Old*, Robert Thomas; *The Words of the Covenant*, Paul Henebury. Also, *Chicago Statement on Biblical Hermeneutics*
[350] e.g. Jer 31:37; 32:37-41; 33:24-26;
[351] 1 Peter 1:10-12

cific *land*.[352] And Noah understood *flood of water* to mean *flood of water*.[353] Similarly, Isaiah took God's words literally.[354] There appears to have been no "distance" between the meaning intended by God and the meaning taken by the aforementioned recipients.

Similarly, in the cases of the angel Gabriel, Mary, Zechariah and Anna quoted in Chapter 6, it is evident their understanding aligned directly with the plain meaning of the words and phrases of the Old Testament writers.

Even giving all due consideration to genre, figures of speech, idioms, analogies, and administrative periods, the concept of *reinterpretation* as wielded by replacementists should be rejected outright.[355]

While the New Testament certainly introduces new information, application and significance, it

---

[352] Gen 13:17; Deut 34:4

[353] Gen 6:17; 7:6

[354] Isa 37:33-37

[355] It should be obvious that *reinterpretation* of formal undertakings is not a legitimate approach, even within our own culture. Who really considers it viable to reinterpret his mortgage agreement or marriage vow? It is true that unclear language can be said to be open to interpretation, but the biblical promises of Israel's restoration are set out in specific and unambiguous language. Further, the very use of the term *reinterpretation* is an acknowledgement that a known original meaning has been replaced by a new, formerly unknown meaning. Few would tolerate such an approach to a mortgage agreement or marriage vow, but if supersessionists are right, it would follow that the God of the Bible holds Himself to a lower standard.

does not change Old Testament meanings.[356] Doing so would render the original meaning false and would show God to be equivocal, His word misleading, and the divine communication project incoherent.[357]

Of course, replacementists will point to the New Testament in their defence of *reinterpretation*. Apparently ignoring the necessary implication that *reinterpretation* renders God deceptive, the claim is made that New Testament writers do indeed reinterpret Old Testament texts. Some of the following devices are employed to support that claim.

---

[356] See *Appendix: Messianic Prophecy* for further comment on the many and varied ways in which the NT quotes or alludes to OT passages.
See also Vlach, *The Old in the New: Understanding How the New Testament Authors Quoted the Old Testament*

[357] Smith: "Whether Gnosticism produced this inversion in biblical theology or was simply a co-inheritor is unclear; but one thing is clear: reversal of the determinative/dependant relationship between the Old and New Testaments, as seen in Gnosticism and amillennialism, is highly destructive both to biblical theology and to our notion of biblical inspiration and canonicity." https://tinyurl.com/2mnu8xhf

II. Proof texting and Decontextualisation

Certain key texts are cited out of context and misinterpreted. By this means, a few lines of text are used to effectively annul large volumes of biblical data and explicit covenantal promises.

The Bible can be used to "prove" anything, but only if context is ignored. Examples of replacementists' proof texts follow.

Romans 4:13

"...that Abraham and his offspring received the promise that he would be heir of the world..."

Replacement theologians of many stripes have in recent decades increasingly relied on Romans 4:13. It is quoted by NT Wright, Gary Burge, Palmer Robertson, Holwerda, four authors of *The Gospel and The Land of Promise*,[358] and by many others, who see this short passage as negating, undermining, transforming or reinterpreting the oft-repeated God-sworn land promise.

---

[358] Walker, Keown, Church, Donaldson

Burge is typical, arguing from Romans 4:13:

…the right to possess the land has now been overturned in Christ.[359]

But such a meaning is foreign to this text, especially when viewed in context.

The word translated *world* is the Greek *kosmos.* Among its possible meanings are *earth* and (*the world's) people.*[360] Of course, context determines meaning.

The promises to Abraham are the context of Romans 4:13 and those promises are multifaceted.[361] One searches in vain for mention of or reference to the land promise in Romans 4. The entire chapter is taken up with the justification and blessing of *persons.*

Among several promises God made to Abraham is that he would be a *father of many nations* and that is indeed specifically mentioned in the immediate context.[362] Thus 4:13 fits very well with that specific promise to Abraham, whereas application to the land promise is forced and non-contextual.

---

[359] *Jesus and The Land*, https://tinyurl.com/4yz6had8

[360] https://www.biblestudytools.com/lexicons/greek/nas/kosmos.html

[361] Including: personal blessing to Abraham, a specific nation from Abraham, blessing to *all* families of the earth, that Abraham would become father of many nations, ownership of the land, etc.

[362] Romans 4:17

Final confirmation that it is not the land promise that is in view, is seen in the verse's construction. Note that the *recipients* differ from the *subject*:[363]

*...**Abraham and his offspring** received the promise...*

The recipients of the promise.

*...that **he** would be heir of the world...*
The subject of the promise.

Abraham and his offspring received the promise but it was *Abraham* alone who would be made *heir of the world* in the sense that he was to become father of many nations, as Paul explained in Romans 4:11, 12, 16 and 17.

Thus Romans 4:13 provides zero support for the assertion that the land promise has been over-turned, transformed, reinterpreted, or annulled.[364]

2 Corinthians 1:20
For all the promises of God find their Yes in him. That is why it is through him that we utter our Amen to God for his glory.

NT Wright was asked the question, *How do you understand the specific Scriptures concerning God's*

---

[363] Nelson Hsieh, *Abraham as Heir of the World*:
https://www.academia.edu/31599166/
[364] See also Vlach: https://sharperiron.org/article/does-romans-413-universalize-israel-s-land-promises

promises to the Jewish people today and also concerning the actual land of Israel?

His response: *I take very seriously what Paul says in 2 Corinthians 1 that all the promises of God find their yes in Christ...*[365]

Wright clearly sees 2 Corinthians 1:20 as meaning there will be no future fulfillment of Israel's promises. But neither the text, nor its context, nor anything else in the New Testament indicates fulfillment of *all* prophecy at Messiah's first advent. Ironically, the text in question speaks of affirmation of God's promises, not their reinterpretation or negation.[366]

Further, Wright's understanding is directly contradicted by Peter. Having been tutored on the coming kingdom by the resurrected Messiah in the days prior,[367] Peter told his Jewish listeners that the fulfilment of certain Old Testament promises awaits Messiah's return.[368]

---

[365] https://www.youtube.com/xR1EKXnJn7s

[366] "...the "Amen" is spoken by us to the glory of God."
Elsewhere Wright explains that he sees the 70AD destruction of the second temple as "not...a different event" to "the Son of Man coming in clouds" (Mk 13:2,4 and 24-27 respectively). He further describes belief in Jesus' literal return to earth ("...the supposed 'heavenly son of man' who would 'come' – i.e. 'return,' downwards to earth, on a literal cloud.") as a "monstrosity." https://tinyurl.com/2p8zysww

[367] Acts 1:3. See comments in Chapter 6.

[368] Acts 3:21

Galatians 3:28-29

There is neither Jew nor Greek, there is neither slave nor free man, there is neither male nor female; for you are all one in Christ Jesus. And if you belong to Christ, then you are Abraham's descendants, heirs according to promise.

This passage has been frequently cited to support a supersessionist position. For example:

The only "Chosen People" and "Chosen nations" are those who have chosen to follow Jesus Christ... ... Galatians 3:28 says there is neither Jew nor Greek, we are all one in Jesus Christ.[369]

...for you are all one in Christ Jesus" (Gal. 3:28). Jesus's "gospel" has overcome all these particularities, made all such distinctions meaningless.[370]

...the church as a new entity, the renewed Israel, now qualitatively distinct from Jew and Greek alike, transcending racial and social barriers (Gal. 3:28)[371]

Thus it is argued that all social, gender, and national distinctions are abolished and Israel's unique covenantal status is done away with. But is that Paul's view?

---

[369] Torba and Isker, *Christian Nationalism* p47

[370] Nirenberg, *Anti-Judaism* p55

[371] NT Wright:
https://www.monergism.com/topics/new-perspective/nt-wright

The context is Paul's argument that it is by faith that anyone can be a *son*[372] and *in Christ,* irrespective of one's status as Jew, Greek, male, female, slave or master. His topic is justification and the spiritual unity that the various parties experience as a result of their being *in Christ.*

Paul elsewhere strongly affirms certain distinctions between male and female and master and servant.[373] He even continues to make limited distinctions in regard to Jewish believers.[374] Clearly, Paul is not teaching that all distinctions are done away with, only that all are justified by the same means, irrespective of race, gender or social standing, and all are united *in Christ.*

Further, Paul's statement that [even non-Jewish believers] *are Abraham's offspring, heirs according to promise* (v29) does nothing to strengthen the replacementists' case. As noted in the preceding comments on Romans 4:13, the promise to Abraham is multifaceted and always included a promise of blessing to non-Jews.

To extrapolate from Galatians 3:28-29 that Israel is somehow stripped of its unique national covenantal promises, or that this somehow implies

---

[372] Gal 3:26
[373] e.g. Eph 5:21-33; 1 Tim 2:8-15; 3:1-2; 1 Pet 3:1-7
1 Tim 6:1,2; Philemon
[374] e.g. Rom 11:5;15:27

that those *in Christ* now constitute *the only chosen people, chosen nation,* or *renewed Israel* is to attribute to Paul a view he does not express here or elsewhere.

In summary, the passage in question deals with the spiritual status and *sonship* of those who believe. It does not address their ethnic, societal, national or gender status.

Galatians 6:16
And as for all who walk by this rule, peace and mercy be upon them, and upon the Israel of God.

On the basis of this text, NT Wright states:

Paul's whole argument is that "the Israel of God" (6:16) consists of all those, Jew and Gentile alike, who believe in Jesus the Messiah.[375]

Thus the short phrase *Israel of God* is used to change the normal biblical definition of Israel, to now include non-Jews, doing away with the covenantal distinction of the Jewish nation.[376]

Martin Luther's view was similar:

The Israel of God are not the physical descendants of Abraham, Isaac, and Israel but those who, with

---

[375] https://ntwrightpage.com/2016/07/12/the-letter-to-the-galatians-exegesis-and-theology/
[376] See Chapter 2

Abraham the believer (Gal 3:9), believe in the promises of God now disclosed in Christ, whether they are Jews or Gentiles.[377]

John Stott stated:

The true Israel today is neither Jews nor Israelis, but believers in the Messiah, even if they are Gentiles...[378]

Similarly, JI Packer:

The church is seen as the family and flock of God... ...his Israel (Gal. 6:16)...[379]

It is quite true that non-Jewish believers are considered *sons of Abraham* through faith.[380] But the Scriptures are quite careful to maintain the distinction between Abraham's spiritual descendants and the nation of Israel, that is, those who are *physically* descended from Abraham *and* Isaac *and* Jacob.

The term Israel or Israelite is used seventy-three times in the New Testament.[381] There is little debate concerning seventy-two of those usages - Israel is used of the descendants of Abraham *and*

---

[377] https://tinyurl.com/4zcutb2v
[378] According to Wagner
[379] https://tinyurl.com/4pju49cy
[380] Rom 4:11; Gal 3:7-9
[381] *Israelology*, Fruchtenbaum, p684-690 lists all 73 usages.

Isaac *and* Jacob, the believing Jewish remnant, the land or nation. And yet replacementists will frequently claim Galatians 6:16 is a reference to both Jewish and non-Jewish believers, thus employing it as a proof text for the notion that the church is the new or true Israel.

This appears to be theological straw-grasping. Are there compelling reasons to accept the replacementists' claim and see this single text as a biblically warranted redefinition of Israel?

The argument rests heavily on the translation of the Greek word *kai,* which means *and* or *in addition to.*

And those who will walk by this rule, peace and mercy be upon them, **and** *upon the Israel of God.*[382]

Replacementists usually prefer the NIV rendering:

Peace and mercy to all who follow this rule, **even** *to the Israel of God.*

Interestingly, the word *kai* occurs three times in this single verse. The NIV editors translated *kai* normally in the first two cases, but, apparently without justification, chose to use the word *even* in the third instance. Why? Presumably because it

---

382 Gal 6:16 NASB

opens the theological door to the idea that Paul is equating Israel with the church.

Translations in which the normal word *and* is used to translate the final *kai* include: KJV, NET, ASV, HCSB, NASB, NKJV, ESV.

What about the broader context? Paul's argument has been urging non-Jews to not submit to circumcision and Mosaic law. He refers to the two groups, Jews and non-Jews, throughout the epistle. Even in the immediately preceding verse he mentions circumcision and uncircumcision. It is in a natural extension of this thought that Paul offers a blessing to both groups in Galatians 6:16:

...*peace and mercy be upon them* (non-Jewish believers Paul has been primarily addressing), *and upon the Israel of God* (believing Jews).

Thus Galatians 6:16 fails to support the claims of replacement theology.[383]

Space will not permit treatment of several other New Testament texts harnessed in support of replacement theology.[384] In each case, immediate or broader context shows such use to be unsound.

---

[383] For a thorough treatment see *Israelology*, p690-699, which cites the work of S Lewis Johnson.

[384] Among them: Matt 21:43; Rom 2:28,29; 9:6; 1 Pet 2:8;9. All are skilfully dealt with in the writings of Sibley, Henebury, Fruchtenbaum, Horner, Vlach, Fretwell and others.

III. NEO-MARCIONISM

The Old Testament text is granted less authority than the New Testament, or is simply ignored. Replacement theology's interpretation of the New Testament becomes the lens through which Old Testament texts must be understood.

Marcion of Sinope (circa 110-160) rejected the Hebrew Scriptures and certain apostolic writings. He considered the God of Old Testament to be a demiurge, distinct and inferior to the God revealed in Jesus. Polycarp, a disciple of the apostle John, apparently recognised the seriousness of Marcion's error and is reported to have called him "the firstborn of Satan".[385]

While Marcion was considered a heretic by the early church his influence was significant and has endured.[386]

In Neo-Marcionism's stronger forms, certain Old Testament passages are simply rejected. For example Naim Ateek, a Palestinian theologian frequent-

---

[385] https://www.britannica.com/topic/Marcionites
[386] A critic may suggest there is not a demonstrable unbroken connection between Marcion and the examples given herein. In any event, the ideas are similar as are the consequences.

ly quoted even by ostensibly evangelical replacement theologians, has said:[387]

When confronted with a difficult passage in the Bible or with a perplexing contemporary event, one needs to ask such simple questions as: Does this fit the picture I have of God that Jesus has revealed to me? ... If it does, then that passage is valid and authoritative. If not, then I can not accept its validity or authority.[388]

In reference to Isaiah 61:5,6, Ateek declares:

This exclusivist text is unacceptable today, whether it has to do with God or people or land. It must be de-Zionized...[389]

There is something refreshingly honest about Ateek's statement. Rather than engage in disingenuous theological manoeuvring to avoid the obvious intention of the text, Ateek simply grants himself magisterial authority and declares the inspired biblical text *unacceptable*. It is clear to Ateek that Isaiah's writings teach Israel's national restoration (and presumably he would view many of the prophetic writings in the same way). As such, the text's plain meaning simply can not stand.

---

[387] e.g. Ateek is referenced favourably *dozens* of times in GLP.
[388] Weekend Herald, New Zealand, December 1-2, 2001
[389] *A Palestinian Christian Cry*, p56. Quoted in *What Should We Think About Israel?* Kindle.

Ateek is a liberal but his position on the obvious meaning of the text is ultimately little different to that of replacementists claiming evangelical credentials.[390] Ateek is unencumbered by the profession of the authority of Scripture and so is able to speak with refreshing transparency. He can unabashedly state that the plain meaning of many Old Testament texts is *unacceptable*.

In its milder forms Neo-Marcionism retains but devalues much of the Old Testament, insisting it can only be understood through replacement theology's interpretation of the New Testament. Thus Old Testament meanings are changed, with all the attendant detrimental implications.[391]

Gary Burge has said:

Too often in my conversations with Christians, they are actually doing Jewish theology. They are working out of Genesis and Ezekiel, and they're working out a theological view of the Middle East which is very much embedded in a Jewish worldview.[392]

---

[390] Many of the most influential supersessionists are identified as conservatives, since they hold to the deity of Messiah, miracles, the virgin conception, resurrection etc. Plainly it would be wrong to call them liberals. It should be apparent, however, that in regard to the issue of Israel, many are *selectively* applying a hermeneutic that is functionally indistinguishable from that of liberalism.

[391] See *Reinterpretation* regarding the resulting incoherence.

[392] http://www.equip.org/audio/hank-hanegraaff-and-special-guest-dr-gary-burge/

It is not difficult to demonstrate that Jesus and his followers were also *working out of* the Old Testament.[393] Indeed, the Old Testament was the *only* Scripture available to Jesus and his first followers. Burge seems to be creating a disjunction between the worldview of Hebrew Scriptures and what he believes is its negation by the New Testament. In contrast this book argues that in the New Testament, the Old Testament operates as a validating authority.[394]

Soulen quite correctly observes that replacement theology *…renders the Hebrew Scriptures largely indecisive for shaping Christian convictions…*[395]

[393] e.g. Jn 5:39,45-47; Acts 17:11
See the texts quoted in Chapter 6, *New Testament Assumptions and Expectations*
[394] See Chapter 6
[395] Soulen, R. *The God of Israel and Christian Theology*

IV. Typology, Allegory and Spiritualization

Israel is reduced to a mere symbol, metaphor, picture or shadow of some future superior reality, typically the church or Jesus. Texts describing Israel's future are said to denote present spiritual realities.

Gary Burge has said:
> *In a word, Jesus spiritualizes The Land.*[396]

Walker sees the land as a metaphor:
> *...as though, in fact, the land were a great advance metaphor for the design of God that his people should eventually bring the whole world into submission to his healing reign.*[397]

Grover Gunn severs Jewish connection to the land by declaring it a temporary typological symbol. He spiritualizes the land promise:
> *I believe the Jewish inhabitation of Palestine in the Old Testament* (sic) *was a temporary typological symbol and pledge of the ultimate eternal inheritance*

---

[396] Burge, *Jesus and the Land*, p395
[397] Walker in GLP, p74, footnote 39, Kindle.

of the saints. I also believe that the land promise ap-
plies to the Christian today in the spiritual rest and
heavenly position that is his in Christ Jesus.[398]

Others go so far as to see Jesus *as* the land:
Jesus is the Promised Land...[399]

Similarly, Hanegraaff:
Jesus is the antitype who fulfills all of the typology
vested in Jerusalem.[400]

And Riddlebarger:
According to amillenarians, this means that Jesus
Christ is the true Israel.[401]

Replacementist Robertson uses *type, shadow* and
picture in this quote:
In the process of redemptive history, a dramatic
movement has been made from type to reality, from
shadow to substance. The land which once was the
specific locale of God's redemptive working served
well within the old covenant as a picture of Paradise
lost and promised.[402]

---

[398] Quoted by Henebury:
https://www.spiritandtruth.org/questions/177.htm?x=x
[399] "Jesus is the Promised Land, the land that we now dwell in."
https://tinyurl.com/53k2jxrp
[400] *The Apocalypse Code,* p223
[401] Riddlebarger: https://tinyurl.com/2f6rjuwc
[402] Quoted both by Horner in *Future Israel* p97 (unfavourably) and
Donaldson in GLP p68 (favourably).

Bass states:

The Israelites, through Abraham, foreshadow the church... [403]

According to Chris Wright:

...it is not a case of abolishing and 'replacing' the realities of Israel and the Old Testament, but of taking them up into a greater reality in the Messiah. Christ does not deprive the believing Jew of anything that belonged to Israel as God's people... [404]

Wright's statement is remarkable. Irrespective of the term used to describe his view, it is one in which Israel is most certainly *deprived* of its distinctive national promises. Only by spiritualizing the text, evacuating words of meaning, and denying the materiality and specificity of the covenantal promises, could Wright make such an assertion. [405]

Each of the above examples is quite consistent with Augustine:

---

[403] https://tinyurl.com/4pc7e62h

[404] https://www.theologicalstudies.org.uk/pdf/jerusalem_wright.pdf
Cited by Church in *GLP*, p153, Kindle (favourably) and by Brown in *Christian Antisemitism*, p148, Kindle (unfavourably).

[405] Earlier in the same chapter Wright says *...nothing in the passages cited requires or supports a national or territorial restoration of the Jews as being necessary...* Gentry and Wellum's approach is similar: *...the inheritance of the 'land' is fulfilled in our Lord Jesus Christ, who brings to completion all of the previous covenants (along with their types and shadows)...*
Kingdom Through Covenant, p713.
See: *V: Christological Interpretation*

For in the Jewish people was figured the Christian people... ...there a shadow, here the body.[406]

Thus the land and the Jews are reduced to type, metaphor, picture or shadow.

BIBLICAL TYPES AND SHADOWS

Types and shadows *are* a biblical reality.[407] Where Scripture uses types they should be embraced. Where unbiblical types and shadows are posited which conflict with explicit scriptural teaching, they are to be rejected.

The book of Hebrews speaks of the tabernacle as being a shadow[408] and addresses at length the superiority of the New covenant to the Mosaic,[409] Messiah's priesthood to that of the Aaronic, and Messiah's sacrifice to those of the Mosaic order.[410] But we do not see the biblical writers treat the Jews and their land as mere types, shadows or metaphors as though they have passed away or are now superseded or irrelevant.

---

[406] https://tinyurl.com/bpaywmew

[407] e.g. Rom 5:14; Col 2:16,17

[408] Heb 8:4

[409] It did not take the writing of Hebrews to learn of the superiority of the new to the Mosaic, it was stated by Jeremiah (Jer 31:32-37).

[410] e.g. Heb 7:11,18,19; 8:6,7

The texts perhaps most frequently cited to argue that Israel is only a type of the church, speak of *events* in Israel's experience, not the people.[411]

Three categories of types or metaphors can be considered:

1. Those that are directly taught in Scripture.

2. Those that, while not taught in Scripture, are consistent with Scripture and serve to illustrate doctrine and reality.[412] Such should be considered tentative and handled with care.

---

[411] e.g. York argues Israel is a type of the church: 'In I Corinthians 10:11 above, the word describing Israel as "an example" to the church is literally "a type." Ironically, Israel itself is the chief type of the church.'
https://tinyurl.com/mrx6c9af
But it is *events* that Paul is citing: "…these *things happened* as examples for us…", "…these *things happened* to them as an example…" 1 Cor 10:6,11
Others appeal to Gal 4 where Paul uses Jerusalem *figuratively* (v24) to illustrate the superiority of the Abrahamic covenant over the Mosaic. He does not, in the process, diminish the significance of the earthly Jerusalem or the Jewish people. Contrary to NT Wright, who seems to overlook Paul's statement that he is speaking *figuratively*, and asserts: *Paul is at pains throughout [Galatians] to distance himself from any geographical or territorial claim; these things are done away with in Christ.* https://ntwrightpage.com/2016/07/12/the-letter-to-the-galatians-exegesis-and-theology/
But the geographical and territorial aspects of the covenant are not Paul's subject matter in Galatians. Also, note Gal 3:15,17 where it is shown the covenant cannot be *set aside.*

[412] e.g. Joseph as a type of Messiah: though at first rejected by his brothers he was later embraced and became their redeemer; though innocent he was falsely accused; while rejected by his own people he gains a non-Jewish bride (the church is predominantly made up of non-Jews); while rejected by his own people, he brought "redemption" to many who were not his people; etc.

3.   Those that are not taught in Scripture and
        contradict explicit biblical teaching. These
        are to be rejected outright.

In this latter category belong the above examples
cited from supersessionists.

As with *reinterpretation,* once embraced as a valid
technique, unbiblical types and shadows can be
used to overturn *any* biblical teaching.

FIGURATIVE LANGUAGE
VERSUS FIGURATIVE INTERPRETATION

It is quite true that the Bible frequently uses figurative language. But as others have observed, there
is a critical distinction between two approaches
that may be taken when one encounters figurative
language:

1.   Recognising that the biblical author has used
        figurative language and understanding his
        meaning accordingly.

2.   Choosing to interpret figuratively.[413]

---

[413] "Whether language is used literally or figuratively is a decision
made by the writer alone, and once he makes this decision, his intent becomes frozen in the text… …It is the interpreter's responsibility simply to recognize what the writer intended to do with the
words he chose. This commitment to consistent literal interpretation maintains a clear distinction between *appreciating figurative
uses of language* and *interpreting figuratively.*" Vlach, TMSJ-
Volume-29-Number-2, p136.

The first approach seeks to honour the writer's intention, making appropriate use of non-figurative biblical material elsewhere in Scripture that addresses the same subject. In the latter approach, however, there is great latitude and the reader's theological presuppositions are free to dictate the text's meaning.

"TREASON TO GOD'S WORD"

The famous English preacher Charles Spurgeon provides interesting commentary on a figurative or spiritualizing interpretation of Ezekiel 37:1-14. Though firmly within a theological tradition dominated by replacement theology, he understood that the restoration of Israel is plainly taught in Scripture.

Spurgeon allowed for an *accommodation* of Ezekiel 37 as *a most striking picture of the restoration of dead souls to spiritual life.*[414] However, he was unafraid to offend his Reformed co-religionists by declaring it nothing less than *treason* to neglect the prophet's primary meaning. In Spurgeon's view, *if words mean anything, first, that there shall be a political restoration of the Jews to their own land and to their own nationality... ...then, secondly, there is in*

---

[414] https://www.ccel.org/ccel/spurgeon/sermons10.xxxvi.html
Elsewhere Spurgeon wrote: "I think we do not attach sufficient importance to the restoration of the Jews. We do not think enough of it. But certainly, if there is anything promised in the Bible, it is this."
https://www.spurgeon.org/resource-library/sermons/the-church-of-christ/

*the text and in the context a most plain declaration
that there shall be a spiritual restoration...*

REAL WORLD IMPACT

When a people group's spiritual significance is diminished, with ownership of their land, city, and history denied or reduced to mere figure, type, or shadow, it easily bleeds into an egregious form of dehumanisation.

This matter moves quickly from the theoretical and abstract to one of great practical consequence when one is confronted with the reality of the reestablished Jewish nation. Is the honest student of Scripture really to believe that modern Israel is merely an inconvenient historical anomaly and that the Jews have outlived their metaphorical, figurative and typological usefulness?

Are those Jews who have been scattered throughout the world for millennia (in fulfillment of direct biblical prophecies, if the text is taken at face value), mere shadows?[415]

And the six million Jews murdered in 1940s Europe, were they merely shadows too?

Such notions are as biblically untenable as they are repugnant.

---

[415] e.g. Deut 4:27; Jer 30:10,11

V. CHRISTOLOGICAL INTERPRETATION

Christ is employed as the lens through which Israel's covenantal promises are reinterpreted. He must be first ethnically cleansed, de-Judaised and otherwise misrepresented before He becomes useful to the supersessionist as a reinterpretive lens.[416]

A valid Christological approach is one in which Messiah retains His identity as King of Israel, the One to restore and regather Israel, destroy their enemies and reign from Jerusalem.[417] The replacementist must presuppose his theology and distort Messiah's mission before using Him to spiritualize the relevant texts.

Of course, for those who claim to base their views on Scripture, severing the link between Messiah and the nation Israel is no small feat. Nor can it be portrayed as merely a theological misstep - rather it is a task that must be approached with considerable intentionality. After all, even in the gospels

---

[416] Christological interpretation in the hands of replacementists could equally be categorised as reinterpretation or spiritualization.
[417] See *Appendix: Messianic Prophecy* for a compilation of messianic titles and offices.

alone, Jesus is referred to as *King of Israel, King of Zion,* or by related terms, twenty-five times.[418]

A clear example appears in the work of Hans LaRondelle, who is quite transparent about his interpretive strategy.[419] He purges Israel's covenants of *ethnic, national,* and *racial* content by imposing his *Christological* and *ecclesiological* (re)interpretation:

Although he does not use the name "Israel," Peter applies Israel's calling now to the church. This is his ecclesiological interpretation of God's covenant with Israel (Ex.19:5,6). This application is the outgrowth of the Christological interpretation of the Messianic prophecies. The ecclesiological application is the necessary extension of the Christological fulfillment. As the body is organically connected to the head, so is the church to the Messiah. The ecclesiological interpretation removes the ethnic and national restrictions of the old covenant. The new covenant people are no longer characterized by race or country, but exclusively by faith in Christ. This can be called Peter's spiritualization of Israel as a "holy nation."[420]

---

[418] Matt 2:2, 6; 21:5; 27:11, 29, 37, 42; Mk 15:2, 9, 12, 18, 26, 32; Luke 23:3, 37, 38; Jn 1:49; 12:13, 14; 18:33, 39: 19:3, 14, 19, 21.

[419] Professor Emeritus of Theology at the Seventh-day Adventist Theological Seminary at Andrews University.

[420] https://www.ministrymagazine.org/archive/1997/06/understanding-israel-in-prophecy

Similarly, WD Davies speaks of *Christological logic* and of *deterritorializing* and *universalising* the promise:

Because the logic of Paul's understanding of Abraham and his personalization of the fulfilment of the promise "in Christ" demanded the deterritorializing of the promise. Salvation was not now bound to the Jewish people centered in the land and living according to the Law: it was "located" not in a place, but in persons in whom grace and faith had their writ. By personalizing the promise "in Christ" Paul universalized it. For Paul, Christ had gathered up the promise into the singularity of his own person. In this way, "the territory" promised was transformed into and fulfilled by the life "in Christ." All this is not made explicit, because Paul did not directly apply himself to the question of the land, but it is implied. In the Christological logic of Paul, the land, like the Law, particular and provisional, had become irrelevant.[421]

Interestingly, the Abrahamic covenant in its original "unreinterpreted" form already includes an unambiguous universal blessing: *through you all the families of the earth will be blessed.*[422] Davies' real agenda seems to be to strip the covenant of its

---

[421] WD Davies, *The Gospel and the Land*. Quoted here: https://creationconcept.info/VH/GLP_WDD_glp.html
Likewise, according to Waltke: *[in the New Testament] The theme of land has been "Christified." A Genesis Commentary*, p72, ePub edition.
[422] Gen 12:3

Jewish and land components through his implementation of so-called *Christological logic.*

Thus Christological interpretation is mustered in an attempt to deny what the Scriptures have made explicit: Christ will one day assume His role as King of Israel, reigning from Jerusalem over restored and regathered Israel.

It is deeply ironic that Christological interpretation, as wielded by replacementists, is so contrary to Christ's own approach to the Old Testament in which the writings of the prophets are taken at face value and seen as the grounds for His messianic claim and future kingdom.[423]

---

[423] See *Chapter 6, Part II,* and *Appendix: Messianic Prophecy*

VI. CONFLATION AND "AMORPHIZATION"[424]

Biblical concepts are stripped of their particularity and detail so as to achieve an amorphous generality. Thereby Israel's covenantal uniqueness is denied and Messiah's identity and destiny are distorted.

T he distinctions and specifics of biblical texts are downplayed in order to yield a de-Judaised, ethnically cleansed universality, as illustrated by the examples below.

THE UNIVERSAL AND THE PARTICULAR

At this juncture, it is important to state that there *is* a valid *universality - all* peoples will be blessed through Abraham and his people - but it is never at the expense of the *particularity* of God's promises.[425] Universality and particularity coexist in the biblical worldview. Romans 11:15 provides us with a strong example:

For if their rejection is the reconciliation of the world, what will their acceptance be but life from the dead?

---

[424] Here coined to mean: *to make shapeless, to strip of detail and specificity, to make a thing's definition vague*
[425] e.g. Gen 12:3b

170

Here the particularity of Israel's experience (specifically her rejection and later acceptance of Messiah), is referenced by Paul in the same sentence as the universal blessing that flows to the world.

Many of the prophetic texts describing Israel's restoration include accounts of the particularity of Israel's position, city and King alongside the universality of blessing to all nations.[426] There is no need to deny Scripture's particularity in order to affirm the universal scope of the blessing available to all mankind.

Replacement theologians seem determined to filter the biblical text through a theological grid that expunges all traces of the specificity and materiality of God's promises to the Jewish people. For example, Messiah's return to the earth is described as being to a particular city, in a particular land, in response to a particular people.[427] Having thus returned, He will rule the whole earth and bring righteousness and justice to all peoples.[428] The specifics of this biblical scenario seem intolerable to many replacement theologians, even though

---

[426] e.g. Isa 2:2-5. Universal peace, justice and brotherhood are not contradicted by Israel's chosenness, rather, they are facilitated thereby.

[427] e.g. Zech 12:10-13:2;14:2-4; Matt 23:37-39

[428] e.g. Zech 8:2-23; 14:9-10,16-21 See also *Appendix: Messianic Prophecy*

they describe the means by which God will bring about a future state of blessing for all peoples.

By God's grace, there is indeed a promised universal blessing, but it is facilitated with and through the particular.

DISTINCTIONS DOWNPLAYED OR DENIED

Conflation or "amorphization" is usually apparent in replacement theology's treatment of Israel and the church. Whether replacementists view the church as the continuation of Israel, her replacement, her extension, her expansion, her completion or her fulfillment, the following biblical distinctions are usually denied or ignored.

ISRAEL	CHURCH
Ethnic group	Includes all ethnicities
Nation	Not a national entity
Land	Landless
Entry by birth	Entry by rebirth
Messiah is King of Nation	Messiah is Head of Body
Believers and unbelievers	Believers
Founded Genesis 15 (12)	Founded Acts 2
Covenants	No covenants of her own

The distinctions between Israel and the church are neither few nor trivial. Thus replacement theology's attempts to equate or conflate Israel with the church is in the first instance a logical fallacy, a form of category mistake. All such attempts do damage to the biblical clarity of the two concepts.

The church has always been the Israel of God and the Israel of God has always been the church.[429]

...there was a Church in Old Testament times; and that the Old Testament and New Testament believers form one Church – the same olive tree (Romans 11).[430]

This conflation of Israel, church and olive tree is only possible if one ignores the specifics of the biblical texts.[431]

Donaldson provides another clear example of conflation and amorphization:

---

[429] https://theaquilareport.com/covenant-theology-is-not-replacement-theology-2/ See Part II, *Prooftexting*

[430] Grier, quoted by Henebury: https://tinyurl.com/n5ufzxv2

[431] See the distinctions between Israel and the church noted above. In addition, equating the olive tree with either Israel or the church is problematic. e.g. natural branches were formerly *in* the olive tree in a state of unbelief (Rom 11:17,19,20) therefore the olive tree cannot be the church. Also, natural branches are described as being *in, out*, then potentially *in* again (Rom 11:17,19,20,23,24). Therefore the olive tree can not be Israel.
It is difficult to be dogmatic about the identity of the olive tree. An apparently viable identification is *provisional place of blessing*. Concerning the olive tree Terence Donaldson says, "The thrust of the verse [i.e. Rom 11:17] is that Gentiles join the Jews who believe, not that they replace the Jews who do not." Quoted by Sibley, *Has The Church Put Israel On The Shelf?* JETS, 58/3, p576.

...the synonymy of eternal life, kingdom of God, salvation, renewal of all things, and the age to come...
...their point of reference is indistinguishable.[432]

To the contrary, the respective points of reference *are* distinguishable. While *Kingdom of God, renewal of all things,* and *the age to come* are indeed closely related concepts, *eternal life* and *salvation* are not their synonyms. Furthermore, *salvation* has several biblical meanings and is frequently not a reference to eternal life.[433]

Conflation of the five terms diminishes Scripture's clarity and serves to obfuscate the dominant biblical meaning of *Kingdom of God,* in which Israel's national restoration is a central and enduring theme.[434]

---

[432] GLP p62, Kindle.

[433] e.g. Ex 14:13; Matt 24:13; Luke 1:71; Acts 27:31; Phil 1:19; 2:12; 1 Tim 2:15; 4:16

[434] See especially, *The Coming Kingdom: What Is the Kingdom and How Is Kingdom Now Theology Changing the Focus of the Church?* Andrew Woods

VII. Fallacious Reasoning

Assertions are made that do not follow from the biblical data.

Fallacious reasoning is evident in the writings of replacement theologians, particularly in their handling of key biblical terms.

People of God

Equivocation is often present in the use of this phrase. *People of God* is a term that can be correctly used of both Israel and of the church.[435] Therefore, according to forms of replacement theology, the church is the new or true Israel. Or, so the reasoning goes, because the church can be described by the term *people of God*, it can no longer apply to Israel.

But the fact that both entities can properly be called *people of God* does not mean they are equivalent or continuous, or that the term no longer applies to Israel. One's mother and one's wife can both be properly described by the term *woman*. This does not mean they are ultimately the same

---

435 e.g. 2 Sam 7:10; Ezek 38:16; Eph 4:12

woman, or that the identity of one is somehow subsumed into the other, or that *woman* can only be used of the one person.

This fallacy usually also entails the undeclared assumption that God can only have one people. Many are inclined to view all biblical data through a lens of personal soteriology. There is, and always has been, only one path to eternal life - by grace through faith, for Jew and Gentile alike. The uniformity of the path to salvation for believers across all ages does not mean there can be no distinction of people groups in God's dealings with mankind. Such a conclusion does not follow from the premise, logically or theologically. In reality God can have a relationship with a nation (of both believers and unbelievers) while also having a relationship of another kind with a new entity of believers from *all* nations.

There is no logical or theological reason to deny the peoplehood of one in favour of the other.

Walker, for example, appears to combine the *one people* fallacy and the either-or fallacy:

...and his true 'people' are a worldwide community, not an ethnic group associated with a particular land.[436]

---

[436] Quoted in GLP, p74, footnote 37.

By preferring *people of God* as a term, supersessionists will frequently forge a path by which to ignore the full implications of the more specific terms *Israel* and *church*.

For example, Church writes:

Nevertheless, while it might be true that the term "Israel" is not applied to the church in the New Testament, there are other considerations. A more fruitful field of enquiry is the identity of the people of God.[437]

Similarly, GE Ladd 1911-1982, a prominent and influential theologian, *instead of... ...referencing "Israel," "nations," "land," and "Zion/Jerusalem,"... ...repeatedly and accommodatingly substitutes "his/ God's people."*[438]

Again, *people of God* is an entirely valid term (when used properly) but the distinctions and specificity of the full biblical vocabulary should be embraced, not avoided.

As already noted, many things that are true of Israel are not true of the church, and many things

---

[437] GLP, p150, Kindle.
[438] According to Horner, *Future Israel*, p219.
Elsewhere, speaking of the church, Ladd wrote: "...our Lord purposed to bring into existence a new people who would take the place of the old Israel..." *The Gospel of the Kingdom, Scriptural Studies in the Kingdom of God*, p112.

that are true of the church are not true of the nation Israel. Israel is an ethnic group and nation consisting of both believers and unbelievers, and one is a Jew by birth. Israel has covenants and land of her own. In contrast, the church consists of believers from all ethnicities, has no land, nationhood, or covenants of her own.

The following diagram helps to illustrate the present relationship and distinction between Israel and the new entity, the church.[439]

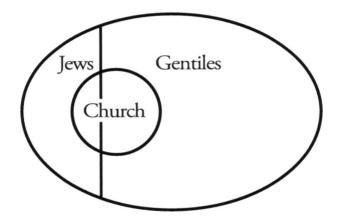

The supersessionists' insistence that there can be only one people of God serves no useful purpose than to sustain a cherished theological misstep and to deny Israel's ultimate national restoration.

___

439 The church is described by Paul as: those in Christ, one new man, God's household. He describes Jewish and Gentile believers united in one entity. Eph 2:13,15,19 Verse 15 uses the word *kainos*: new as to form or quality.

FATHER ABRAHAM

A similar equivocation is seen in supersessionists' handling of the biblical data concerning Abraham's fatherhood.

Abraham is a father of Israel and is also seen as father of all who believe.[440] So, it is argued, the church has replaced or is the continuation/expansion/fulfillment/extension/completion of Israel.

For example, Palestinian Bishop Riah Abu El-Assal said:

We are the true Israel... ...no one can deny me the right to inherit the promises, and after all the promises were first given to Abraham and Abraham is never spoken of in the Bible as a Jew. He is the father of the faithful.[441]

According to Donaldson:

The people of God are now those who are in Christ, the true Israel. These are the children of God (Gal 3:26), Abraham's offspring, and heirs according to the promise (Gal 3:29).[442]

---

[440] Gen 12:2; Rom 4:11,12; Gal 3:6-9
[441] http://archive.spectator.co.uk/article/16th-february-2002/14/christians-who-hate-the-jews
[442] GLP, p71

It appears that he is arguing:
people of God = true Israel = those in Christ = Abraham's offspring = children of God

In our earlier treatment of Galatians 6:16 it was shown that *Israel* is never used of non-Jews.[443] And the equivocation often associated with supersessionists' use of *people of God* is addressed in the preceding pages.

A false equivalence is seen in failing to distinguish the two concepts: Abraham as the *physical* father of the nation Israel; and Abraham as the *spiritual* father of *all* who believe. Biblically, he is father to both entities, but in two different senses.

The confusion is further compounded by disregard of the normal biblical definition of the people of Israel: descendants of Abraham *and* Isaac *and* Jacob, not merely descendants of Abraham.[444]

Each of the above terms should be used with due consideration to their Scriptural meanings, rather than loosely applied in service of a supersessionist framework.

---

[443] See Part II, *Proof Texting and Decontextualisation*
[444] See Chapter 2, *Who Is Israel?*

The Land
Colin Chapman asserts:

…there is only one clear and obvious reference to the land in his [Jesus'] teaching.[445]

This remarkable claim is both fallacious and incorrect. The specific term *land* need not be present for there to be a "clear and obvious reference to the land."[446] Jesus' teaching referenced Jerusalem a number of times and readers will recognise that Jerusalem is part of, and indeed the very centre of the land.[447] Furthermore, the land is the "clear and obvious" context of major portions of Messiah's teachings.[448]

Similarly, Church claims:

There is not one reference to the land of Israel in the writings of Paul, James, Peter, or Jude, or in the Book of Revelation.[449]

---

[445] *Whose Promised Land?*, Chapman 2002, p154. Chapman has in mind Matt 5.

[446] Chapman's argument is certainly a non sequitur and is perhaps a Fallacy of Presumption. The assumption is made that in order to show that a particular subject matter is referenced in a text, a specific term must be present.

[447] Matt 23:37; Lk 13:34

[448] Matt 24:15-20; Mk 13:14-19; Luke 21:20-24

[449] GLP, p49, Kindle.

One need only mention Paul's references to the covenants and promises.[450] The divine covenants include *known, specific and unambiguous* content in which the land serves as an unmistakably essential component. Only those who have embraced reinterpretation or some of the other concepts outlined in this section, can construe such solemn undertakings as not referencing the land.

[450] Rom 9:4;15:8;11:26,27 (note also *Zion* in 11:26); 2 Cor 1:20
Likewise, Chapman quotes Rom 9:1-5 in its entirety and yet despite the explicit mention of Israel's *covenants* and *promises,* he sees this as evidence that "land is conspicuous by its absence in the letters of Paul." *Whose Promised Land?*, Chapman 2002, p175.

VIII. Theological Override

A theological framework or motif is presupposed, to which all biblical data must submit. Having embraced a system of theology, that system becomes the authoritative lens through which all biblical data is read.

Systematic theology: a wonderful servant but a cruel master

As a tool for organising biblical data, systematic theology is most helpful. However, when authority shifts from Scripture to an uninspired theological system, it becomes the filter through which Scripture is read and thus can become deeply misleading.

Theological systems tend to take on a life of their own. Once established, proponents often make further developments based on the system's own propositions rather than induction from Scripture.[451] Scripture should function as the corrective authority to all theological systems. Even

---

[451] All theological systems seem to exhibit this tendency, to a greater or lesser degree.

the core tenets of a system must be subject to modification or rejection when a plain reading of Scripture shows it to be necessary.

Albertus Pieters provides a vivid example of *theological override*. Despite the New covenant explicitly guaranteeing Israel's national perpetuity, Pieters stated:[452]

God willed that after the institution of the New Covenant there should no longer be any Jewish people in the world... "[453]

Pieters evidently felt able to directly contradict an explicit declaration of Scripture on the basis of his prior theological commitment.

Henebury points out another example:

---

[452] Jer 31:36

[453] *The Seed of Abraham,* Pieters
Elsewhere Pieters is remarkably frank that he and *the mass of Christian scholars* are denying the *ordinary sense, as other Scriptures are interpreted* and substituting instead a *spiritualization.*
"The question whether the Old Testament prophecies concerning the people of God must be interpreted in their ordinary sense, as other Scriptures are interpreted, or can properly be applied to the Christian Church, is called the question of spiritualization of prophecy. This is one of the major problems in biblical interpretation, and confronts everyone who makes a serious study of the Word of God. It is one of the chief keys to the difference of opinion between Premillenarians and the mass of Christian scholars. The former reject such spiritualization, the latter employ it; and as long as there is no agreement on this point the debate is interminable and fruitless." Quoted in *Vital Theological Issues,* Zuck, p188.
One wishes that other supersessionists were equally transparent.

(Covenant theologian) Gertsner's problem is that to him, the covenant of grace is so all-encompassing it blots out the wording of Scripture... There simply is no such thing as "the covenant of grace" on the pages of Scripture.[454]

Similarly, Van Gemeren observes that one of his fellow Reformed theologians is willing to allow his theological system to override Scripture:

The authority of the OT as well as of the NT seems to be sacrificed out of concern for unity, harmony, and systemization.[455]

Boettner provides another stark example. Despite unambiguous biblical statements to the contrary, Boettner's theological framework emboldens him to declare:

...the Old Covenant, which we have in the first part of our Bibles in the Old Testament, was made exclusively with the nation of Israel. ...it now has been replaced by the New Covenant, which we call the New Testament, which was made exclusively with the church."[456]

---

[454] https://tinyurl.com/ykysp7wf

[455] Van Gemeren critiquing Herman Bavinck. Quoted by Horner in *Future Israel*, p313

[456] Boettner, *The Meaning of the Millennium: Four Views*, ed. Robert G. Clouse, 1977). Jer 31:31 and Heb 8:8 both declare the NC is made with *Israel and Judah,* not *the church.* Boettner adds further confusion by conflating *New Covenant* and *New Testament*, the latter being a term applied to the writings of the apostles and their associates, probably by Tertullian, many years later.

While *theological override* is evident in multiple fields of Christian thought, it is never more so than in regard to the abundant biblical material relating to Israel's restoration.

Communities of believers are inclined to form echo chambers around common theological positions. Sometimes even minor dissent comes at the cost of unannounced banishment from the inner circle of fellowship. This phenomenon compounds the problem of *theological override,* providing a strong psychological disincentive to the healthy questioning of long-held tradition.

If it is true that Scripture is the final authority, as evangelicals usually profess, then all theological assumptions must remain subject to its scrutiny, no matter how widely held, time-honoured or cherished those views may be.[457]

---

[457] The writer suspects that the vast variation of views within Christendom, even amongst those professing a high view of Scripture, is in part due to the phenomenon of theological override. Over time, foundational theological missteps are built upon until a formidable structure of interdependent ideas exists. This ultimately becomes authoritative in practice, although this is seldom explicitly acknowledged.

APPENDICES

*These are my words
that I spoke to you
while I was still with you,
that everything written about
me in the law of Moses and
the prophets and the psalms
must be fulfilled.*

Luke 24:44

MESSIANIC PROPHECY

MESSIAH IN THE HEBREW SCRIPTURES

W hy include an appendix on messianic prophecy in a relatively short book about Israel's place in the biblical worldview? Because Israel and the Messiah are inextricably linked.

Faithfully handling the biblical data on Messiah takes one a long way toward a correct understanding of the place of Israel. Conversely, writing Israel out of the biblical worldview - which replacement theology in its multiple forms does, to a lesser or greater extent - inevitably distorts the biblical portrait of Messiah. It is hoped that the prophecies cited in this appendix will ably demonstrate that contention.[458]

Liberal scholarship rejects the concept of direct messianic prediction in the Old Testament.[459] An increasing number of ostensibly evangelical theologians have embraced this view, preferring approaches which downplay or deny the necessarily supernatural prophetic nature of many of the texts cited in this appendix.[460] According to Rydelnik, denial of Old Testament messianic prediction by evangelicals is *for the sake of respectability in the academy or acceptance among critical scholarship*.[461] The "enlightenment" of certain portions of the academy was well described by AT Robertson: *Je-*

---

[458] Of course, replacementists will appeal to *reinterpretation* and the various other techniques outlined in Part II in an attempt to avoid the implications of the various prophecies. But, taken at face value, many of these prophecies do indeed place Messiah firmly in an Israel setting from which He can not be extracted.

[459] German critical scholarship played a major role in "removing" the Messiah from the OT. e.g. "Herder maintained that it was a mistake to believe that the Hebrew prophets foretold the distant future. Eichhorn was even more decisive in his rejection of all messianic predictions. He saw this is as a dogmatic and theological imposition on the biblical text... ...In 1793 he boasted 'The last three decades have erased the Messiah from the Old Testament'."
Rydelnik, *The Moody Handbook of Messianic Prophecy* (hereafter MHMP), p74

[460] As Sailhamer says (quoted by Rydelnik): "...the OT does not only predict the coming of a Messiah. It also describes and identifies that Messiah." *MHMP*, p82. Pages 73-92 provide a useful summary of approaches.

[461] *The Messianic Hope: Is The Hebrew Bible Really Messianic?*
https://tinyurl.com/mjaz8ce5

sus found himself in the Old Testament, a thing that some modern scholars do not seem to be able to do.[462]

Jesus clearly held His hearers accountable on the basis of Old Testament prophecy.[463] This necessarily implies the binding validity of direct messianic prediction. Thus, denial of messianic prophecy strikes a significant blow to the coherence of the biblical message.

Many of the criticisms of replacement theology offered in this work equally apply to a denial of direct messianic prediction in the Old Testament. The two issues are inextricably connected - Messiah is, after all, the central figure in Old Testament predictions of Israel's restoration. To deny the validity of messianic prediction is to undermine Israel's restoration. Conversely, to deny the predictions of Israel's restoration is to truncate and distort details of Messiah's mission.[464]

Peter describes the way Old Testament prophets sought to understand the details of Messiah's "sufferings and glory" that they themselves had recorded under the inspiration of the Holy

---

[462] In AT Robertson's commentary on Luke 24:47:
https://tinyurl.com/c7za2pxc
Quoted in *MHMP*, p25, Kindle
[463] e.g. Jn 5:39,45-47; Luke 24:25-27,44.
[464] e.g. Isa 11:11-12 and Jer 23:6,7 see Messiah regathering Israel. Zeph 3:15 and Mal 3:3,4 see Messiah in the midst of regathered Israel.

Spirit.[465] To deny the predictive nature of those texts is to deny those prophets' self-awareness as prophets and to declare Peter mistaken.

RABBINIC EXPECTATION

Interestingly, many of the Old Testament prophecies that conservative Christians today see as predictions of Messiah were also seen as messianic by ancient rabbis. Certainly, Jesus was not recognised as Messiah by those rabbinic authorities but nonetheless the evidence is strong that many key texts were viewed as messianic.[466] Indeed, the ancient rabbis believed the coming of the Messiah to be a supremely important theme in the writings of the prophets. This is evident in the oft-quoted statement:

Every prophet only prophesied for the days of the Messiah...[467]

It is also seen in Rambam's thirteen principles, which he taught must be believed in order for one to be considered a Jew.[468] The twelfth reads:

---

[465] 1 Pet 1:10-11.

[466] See *The Messiah Texts,* Raphael Patai. Or from a believing scholar: *What The Rabbonim Say About Moshiach,* Douglas Pyle.

[467] Berakhot 34b

[468] Rambam is an acronym for Rabbi Moshe ben Maimon, 1135(?)-1204, a highly significant figure in Judaism.

I believe with complete faith in the coming of Mashiach, and although he may tarry, nevertheless, I wait every day for him to come.[469]

WHAT IS FULFILLMENT?

At this juncture it is important to point out that the New Testament quotes or alludes to Old Testament texts in various ways, only a minority of which constitute concrete fulfillment of direct messianic prediction.[470] Mere mention or allusion to an Old Testament text by a New Testament writer is insufficient to mark a fulfillment of predictive prophecy.[471]

Even modern English speakers can make allusions without a listener assuming more than that a similarity or parallel is being noted. For exam-

---

[469] https://www.sefaria.org/sheets/260872

[470] Zuck lists ten distinct categories of NT usage of OT texts in *Basic Bible Interpretation, A Practical Guide to Discovering Biblical Truth.* Vlach's, *The Old in the New: Understanding How the New Testament Authors Quoted the Old Testament* is a very good treatment of this topic.
Even the presence of the word *fulfill* in the English NT does not necessarily indicate realisation of an OT prediction. The Greek word *pleroo* has a *much* broader range of meaning than the English word *fulfill/fulfillment* by which it is frequently translated.
It is acknowledged that many writers use the word *fulfillment* more loosely. The point here is not to argue for a narrow use of the term *fulfilment* but simply to recognise the distinction between actual realisation of OT predictions and other kinds of NT usage of OT texts.

[471] e.g. Matt 2:17,18. The case of Jn 19:37 could be understood as fulfillment of a specific *part* of the prediction (piercing) but not the "looking". In the context of Zech 12:10, the "looking" is a future action by "the house of David and the inhabitants of Jerusalem" under the influence of the Holy Spirit, following the events of Zech 12:1-9.

ple, if one says *"the writing is on the wall for [a current political leader]"*, it is not taken to mean that the speaker sees the current situation as a fulfillment of Daniel 5:5. Rather, it is understood that a motif is borrowed to suggest coming judgement or removal from office.

It is *direct correspondence* between the details of an Old Testament predicted event or person and the details of the New Testament event or person that gives the reader confidence to identify a prediction's fulfillment.

Those Old Testament messianic predictions that were fulfilled at Jesus' first coming, were fulfilled *as written*. To be consistent, it should be recognised that the remaining predictions will also be fulfilled *as written*.

Some theologians instead insist that all messianic predictions were fulfilled at Messiah's first coming. To sustain such a view, one must negate, obfuscate or reinterpret the plain meaning of the texts in question.[472] This has significant negative implications for the integrity and coherence of the biblical message.

---

[472] See Part II re the incoherence and untenability of replacement theology's approach to this matter.

A Selection of Old Testament Messianic Predictions

What follows is a compilation of messianic prophecies, titles or descriptions, one for each of the twenty-two letters of the Hebrew alphabet.[473]

What is the special theological significance of such a compilation? There is none. This acrostic is merely an interesting device around which to create a compilation.[474] That such a collection is possible does demonstrate, however, just how prominent messianic prediction is in the Old Testament.

Each title, prediction or description is provided in English and Hebrew along with a short summary of the data provided by the passage and its context. Where a passage was considered messianic by rabbinic authorities, this is noted. Several related Old Testament passages are also provided.

When taken as a whole, a comprehensive picture of Messiah's identity and career comes into view. What should be obvious to any reader is that Messiah's connection to Israel is inviolable.

---

[473] This is a minor revision of the author's 2008 project *Messiah Comes: Messiah in the Hebrew Scriptures*
https://www.messiah.com.es
[474] Readers will be aware that Psalm 119 is an acrostic, lines of each stanza beginning with a particular letter of the Hebrew alphabet.

MAN OF SORROWS
איש מכאבות

He was despised and rejected by men, a man of sorrows, and familiar with suffering. Like one from whom men hide their faces he was despised, and we esteemed him not.

Isaiah 53:3

SUMMARY: Messiah will be despised and rejected by His own people and will be familiar with sorrow and grief. Though innocent, He will bear the sins of His people who will consider Him guilty, stricken by God.

Isaiah 52:13-53:12 is said by most modern rabbis to be speaking of Israel, not the Messiah. There is strong evidence, however, that the text was considered messianic by many (or most) rabbinic authorities, until the time of Rashi, 1040-1105.[475] Indeed, leading Talmudic scholar Daniel Boyarin wrote in 2012:

The early modern Kabbalist Rabbi Moshe Alshekh, also a spotlessly "orthodox" rabbinite teacher, writes, "I may remark, then, that our Rabbis with one voice accept and affirm the opinion that the prophet is

---

[475] *What the Rabbonim Say About Moshiach*, Pyle (hereafter WRSM), pages 9,12,56,57
Rashi is the acronym for Rabbi Shlomo Yitzchaki

speaking of the King Messiah, and we ourselves also adhere to the same view." The intellectual giant of Spanish Jewry, Rabbi Moses ben Nahman, concedes that according to the midrash and the rabbis of the Talmud, Isaiah 53 is entirely about the Messiah, but he dissents.[476]

It is difficult to overstate the significance of Isaiah 52:13-53:12.[477] Arguably, more is revealed about Messiah in this single passage than in any other messianic passage in the Old Testament. Indeed, these fifteen verses speak of Messiah's humiliation and rejection,[478] innocence,[479] death,[480] resurrection[481] and exaltation.[482] Also made clear is that Messiah will be a sin bearer and substitute.[483]

[476] Boyarin. *The Jewish Gospels*, Kindle, location 2110-2116

[477] German scholar Franz Delitzsch 1813-1890 said: "How many are there whose eyes have been opened when reading this 'golden passional of the Old Testament evangelist,' as Polycarp the Lysian calls it!"
Biblical Commentary on the Prophecies of Isaiah, Volume 2, Delitzsch, p303

[478] Isa 52:14; 53:2-4

[479] Isa 53:9 The innocence of the referent is a strong indicator that it is *not* the nation Israel in view. Isaiah spent much time addressing Israel's sins.

[480] Isa 53:9,10,12

[481] Isa 53:10,11

[482] Isa 52:13; 53:12

[483] Isa 53:4-6,8,10,12

Unsurprisingly, Isaiah 53 continues to be significantly contested in Jewish circles, and especially in any Jewish-Christian dialogue.[484]

Most of Isaiah 53 was fulfilled at Jesus' first coming.[485]

Three of the texts chosen for this compilation are drawn from this passage.

Texts related to Isaiah 53:3 include: Isaiah 49:7; 50:6; 53:7; Psalm 22:16.

---

[484] According to Dovid Rosenzweig: "For modern Jews, the fifty third chapter of Isaiah has been the most controversial and debated chapter of the Tanakh. The controversy surrounds the identity of whom Isaiah is referring to." In personal communication.

[485] e.g. Matt 12:24; 27:41-44

SON OF DAVID
בן דוד

For to us a child is born, to us a son is given, and the government will be on his shoulders. And he will be called Wonderful Counselor, Mighty God, Everlasting Father, Prince of Peace. Of the increase of his government and peace there will be no end.

He will reign on David's throne and over his kingdom, establishing and upholding it with justice and righteousness from that time on and forever. The zeal of the LORD Almighty will accomplish this.

Isaiah 9:6-7[486]

SUMMARY: Messiah will be a descendant of King David. His Kingdom will be everlasting and characterized by righteousness, justice and peace. He will be a man and yet will be given divine titles.

Isaiah 9 was considered messianic in some rab-

---

[486] In the Hebrew text, Isaiah 9:5,6

binic writings.[487]

Portions of this prophecy were fulfilled at Messiah's first coming.[488] The establishment of His kingdom and His reign from David's throne awaits future fulfillment.

Related texts include: Jeremiah 23:5; 33:17; Isaiah 7:14; 11:1-12; Daniel 7:13; 1 Chronicles 17:13; Proverbs 30:4; Psalm 16:10.

---

[487] *Answering Jewish Objections to Jesus, Volume 3*, Michael Brown, endnote 86.
Also, *The Life and Times of Jesus The Messiah*, Edersheim, Appendix 9: *List of Old Testament Passages Messianically Applied in Rabbinic Writings* (hereafter LTJM, App9) "Is. ix. 6 is expressly applied to the Messiah in the Targum…"
[488] Luke 1:31-33;2:6-7
See Jonathan Sarfati's commentary: https://www.messiah.com.es/isaiah-9

REDEEMER
גואל

"The Redeemer will come to Zion, to those in Jacob who repent of their sins," declares the LORD.

Isaiah 59:20

SUMMARY: Messiah will come to Zion. He will bring redemption for all those who turn away from their sin.

The immediate context speaks of Israel's restoration, making it clear that this passage awaits future fulfillment.

This passage was considered messianic by Ibn Ezra, and others.[489]

Related texts include: Job 19:26; Isaiah 53:5; Zechariah 14:3-4; Psalm 130:8.

---

[489] LTJM, App9: "Is. lix. 19, 20, is applied to Messianic times in Sanh. 98 *a*. In Pesiqta 166 *b* it is similarly applied,…"

JUDGE OF NATIONS
דין גוים

He will judge the nations, heaping up the dead and crushing the rulers of the whole earth.

Psalms 110:6

SUMMARY: Messiah will judge the nations and utterly destroy Israel's enemies. In anger He will strike the world's rulers.

This prediction awaits fulfillment at Messiah's return.

Psalm 110 was considered to be messianic in many rabbinic writings.[490]

Related texts include: Numbers 24:8b,17-20; Psalm 2:8-12; 110:1,2; Isaiah 60:10-14; Joel 3:1-3,12; Zechariah 12:9,10; 14:3-4.

---

[490] LTJM, App9: "Ps. cx. is throughout applied to the Messiah…"

FIRSTBORN SON
הבכור

And I will pour out on the house of David and the inhabitants of Jerusalem a spirit of grace and supplication. They will look to me, the one they have pierced, and they will mourn for him as one mourns for an only child, and grieve bitterly for him as one grieves for a firstborn son.

Zechariah 12:10

SUMMARY: Messiah will be One over whom the house of David and inhabitants of Jerusalem mourn, following a time of great distress. He will be recognized as the One whom they have pierced.

The context makes clear that this prediction awaits fulfillment at Messiah's return.

It was considered messianic according to Edersheim.[491]

Related texts include: Genesis 3:15; Isaiah 7:14; 9:6; 49:3; Proverbs 30:4.

---

[491] LTJM, App9: "Zech. xii. 10 is applied to the Messiah the Son of Joseph in the Talmud (Sukk. 52 a)…"

AND RIDING ON A DONKEY
ורכב על חמור

Rejoice greatly, Daughter Zion! Shout, Daughter Jerusalem! See, your king comes to you, righteous and victorious, lowly and riding on a donkey, on a colt, the foal of a donkey.

Zechariah 9:9

SUMMARY: Messiah will enter Jerusalem as Israel's king, riding on a donkey. He will be gentle and righteous and will bring salvation to His people.

This prediction was fulfilled at Messiah's first coming.[492] The verses immediately following will be fulfilled at His return.

Zechariah 9:9 was, and is, widely held to be messianic.[493]

Related texts include: Genesis 49:10,11 and Psalm 118:26.

---

[492] Matt 21:1-9; Mk 11:1-10
[493] LTJM, App9: "The verse is also Messianically quoted in Sanh. 98 a, in Pirqé de R. Eliez. c. 31, and in several of the Midrashim." Rashi held this text to be messianic. *WRSM*, p13

SEED OF THE WOMAN
זרע האישה

And I will put enmity between you and the woman, and between your offspring and hers; he will crush your head, and you will crush his heel.

Genesis 3:15

SUMMARY: Messiah will be born of a woman and will be at enmity with Satan's seed. Though Messiah will be wounded by Satan, He will ultimately inflict a fatal blow on His adversary.[494]

The is the first messianic prophecy and it sets out the cosmic drama in summary form. It is the framework   upon which subsequent prophecy builds.[495]

Later biblical data suggests that both comings of Messiah are in view in this enigmatic prophecy. At

---

[494] Not all conservative commentators view this text as messianic, though perhaps a majority do. It is sometimes referred to as *protoevangelium*, first gospel. For a suggested list of defences of the messianic view see *Answering Jewish Objections to Jesus, Volume 3*, Brown, endnote 18.

[495] "...the 'mother prophecy' that gave birth to all the rest of the promises." "The *protoevangelium* is a presentation of the entire history of humanity in miniature." *The Messiah in the Old Testament*, Kaiser, p38,41. (Hereafter MIOT.)

His first coming, Messiah was "struck" but in the process achieved victory over Satan and his associates by the cross.[496] Messiah will ultimately crush Satan's head upon His return.

Genesis 3:15 was considered messianic in several rabbinic sources.[497]

Related texts include: Isaiah 7:14; 9:6-7 and 53:5.

---

[496] Col 2:15

[497] LTJM, App9: "*Gen iii*. 15. This well-known passage is paraphrased, with express reference to the Messiah, in the Targum Pseudo Jonathan and the so-called Jerusalem Targum."
Kaiser, quoting Martin, shows that the translators of the LXX likely viewed this passage as messianic. MIOT, p40

SHOOT FROM
THE STUMP OF JESSE
חטר מגזע ישי

A shoot will come up from the stump of Jesse;
from his roots a Branch will bear fruit.

Isaiah 11:1

SUMMARY: Messiah will arise from the lineage of Jesse, at a time when the Davidic dynasty seems finished. The Spirit of God will rest upon Him and He will be a just judge.

Messiah was born into the line of David.[498] The Holy Spirit rested upon Him.[499] The remainder of Isaiah 11 provides a detailed description of many of the activities of His return, including the re-gathering of Israel and the establishment of His kingdom.

This prophecy was widely seen as messianic.[500]

Related texts include: Isaiah 4:2; 9:6,7; 53:2 and Jeremiah 23:5; 33:15.

---

[498] Luke 1:31-33

[499] Matt 3:16; Jn 3:34

[500] LTJM, App9: "Is. xi., as will readily be believed, is Messianically interpreted in Jewish writings. Thus, to begin with in the Targum on verses 1 and 6; in the Talmud (Jer. Berach. 5 a and Sanh. 93 b); and in a number of passages in the Midrashim…"

PURIFIER OF
THE SONS OF LEVI
טהר את בני לוי

He will sit as a refiner and purifier of silver; he will purify the Levites and refine them like gold and silver. Then the LORD will have men who will bring offerings in righteousness...

Malachi 3:3

SUMMARY: Messiah will refine and purify the Levites just as the refiner's fire purifies gold or silver. Then there will be men to offer righteous sacrifices in Jerusalem.

The fulfillment of this prediction awaits Messiah's return.

This prophecy was seen as messianic by Moses Maimonides.[501]

Related texts include: Psalm 132:16; Isaiah 4:4; Ezekiel 44:15; Zechariah 13:1-5,7-9.

---

[501] *The Messiah Texts*, Raphael Patai, p326

ISRAEL
ישראל

He said to me, "You are my servant, Israel, in whom I will display my splendour."

Isaiah 49:3

SUMMARY: Messiah will be God's servant, the supreme Israelite through whom He will display His splendour. He will restore the tribes of Jacob, and become a light to the non-Jewish world, bringing salvation to the far reaches of the earth.

This prophecy relates to both Messiah's first coming and His return.

Related texts include: Isaiah 42:1; 52:13; Jeremiah 23:5-8

EXCURSUS

A cursory reading of this text would suggest that *Israel* in Isaiah 49:3 is a reference to the nation. However, a closer examination indicates it is the Messiah who is in view.

The immediate context, verses 1-7, could only apply to one particular Israelite. He is "formed in the womb", is appointed "to bring Jacob back to him and gather Israel to himself".[502] Additionally, He is further distinguished from the nation by being "despised and abhorred by the nation."[503]

These descriptions make little sense as a reference to the whole nation but all fit the Messiah very well.[504] He is the supreme Israelite, the centre of the nation, Israel's King and Redeemer, and the One who will ultimately restore and regather Israel.

Incidentally, also visible in this passage is the faithful remnant of Israel: "those of Israel I have kept".[505]

But doesn't the observation that Messiah is given the title *Israel* lend weight to the contentions of replacementists, that all the promises to Israel are

---

[502] Isaiah 49:5

[503] Isaiah 49:7 See also Isa 53:3,4

[504] Brown concurs: 'Significantly, in 49:1-6, the Servant, who is clearly an individual, is called "Israel" in v. 3 but has the mission of restoring Jacob and regathering Israel in vv. 5-6. ...remember that Israel was first a personal name before being a corporate name, just as was the case with Jacob, so a personal use of the name in 49:3 is hardly inappropriate."
MHMP, p963, Kindle.
Also Chisholm: 'So the Servant is Israel in some sense, while at the same time being distinct from exiled Israel. He is best identified as an ideal Israel who is all that God intended the nation to be, in contrast to exiled Israel, which failed to fulfill God's purposes.' *MHMP*, p946, Kindle.

[505] Isaiah 49:6 The faithful subgroup, the remnant of Israel, is also referenced in Isa 10:20-22; Jer 31:7; Rom 2:29; 9:6; 11:5; Gal 6:16.

fulfilled in Jesus Himself, and that Jesus "is the promised land" or "is the true Israel"?[506]

Not at all.

The Jesus of replacement theology is an ethnically-cleansed and de-Judaized distortion of the genuine. He is a theological fabrication and an impostor who will never complete the mission given to the biblical Messiah. The deeply flawed Christology of replacement theology portrays an individual who does not now, nor ever will, satisfy the criteria set out in Isaiah 49, or in many of the other texts referenced in this appendix.

---

[506] Especially as described in Part II, *IV Typology, Allegory and Spiritualization* and *V Christological Interpretation*
https://tinyurl.com/53k2jxrp
Riddlebarger: https://tinyurl.com/2f6rjuwc

STAR FROM JACOB
כוכב מיעקב

I see him, but not now; I behold him, but not near; a star shall come forth from Jacob, a sceptre shall rise from Israel, and shall crush through the forehead of Moab, and tear down all the sons of Sheth.

Numbers 24:17

SUMMARY: Messiah will one day arise from Israel. He will be a royal ruler and will destroy Israel's ancient enemies.

Although Messiah has indeed arisen from Jacob's line, the subjugation of Israel's enemies awaits Messiah's return.

This passage was seen as messianic by many rabbinic authorities.[507]

Related texts include: Genesis 3:15; 49:10; Psalm 110:6; Isaiah 9:6-7; Micah 5:2.

---

[507] LTJM, App9: "*Num. xxiv.* 17 Balaam's prediction of the Star and Sceptre is referred to the Messiah in the Targum Onkelos and the Targum Pseudo-Jonathan, as well as in Jer. Taan. iv. 8; Deb. R. 1; Midr. on Lament. ii. 2. Similarly *verses 20 and 24* of that prophecy are ascribed in the Targum Pseudo-Jon. to the Messiah."
Interestingly, Simon bar Koseba, a military leader in the second Jewish revolt 132-135, was declared to be the Messiah by Rabbi Akiva who gave him the title bar Kokhba (son of the star), in accordance with this prophecy. Bar Kochba was later killed and the revolt was crushed.

TO BE RULER OVER ISRAEL
להיות מושל בישראל

But you, Bethlehem Ephrathah, though you are small among the clans of Judah, out of you will come for me one who will be ruler over Israel, whose origins are from of old, from the days of eternity.

Micah 5:2[508]

SUMMARY: Messiah will come forth from Bethlehem, a small town in Judah. He will have eternal origins and will become ruler of Israel.

Messiah, the God-man, was born in Bethlehem.[509] Not until He returns will He begin His rule over Israel.

This prophecy was viewed as messianic by Rashi and others.[510]

Related texts include: Genesis 49:10; Numbers 24:17-20; Isaiah 9:6; Jeremiah 23:5; Daniel 9:24-27.

---

[508] Micah 5:1 in the Hebrew text.

[509] Matt 2:1; Luke 2:7

[510] *Answering Jewish Objections to Jesus, Volume 3*, Michael Brown p39

LTJM, App9: "The well-know passage, Micah v. 2, is admittedly Messianic. So in the Targum, in the Pirqé de R. Eliez. c. 3, and by later Rabbis."

MESSIAH THE PRINCE
משיח נגיד

So you are to know and discern that from the issuing of a decree to restore and rebuild Jerusalem until Messiah the Prince there will be seven sevens and sixty-two sevens...

Daniel 9:25

SUMMARY: Messiah will be a ruler. He will appear at a set time in Israel's history and must be executed before the second temple is destroyed.

Messiah's first coming was in accordance with Daniel's timetable.[511] Messiah was crucified approximately forty years prior to the second temple's destruction by the Romans.

This prophecy was apparently seen as revealing the timing of Messiah's coming.[512]

Related texts include: Genesis 49:10; Isaiah 53:4-12; Jeremiah 23:5,6; Micah 5:2.

---

[511] See Zuber's commentary on Dan 9:24-27 in *MHMP*. Also, Fruchtenbaum's commentary: https://www.messiah.com.es/daniel-9
[512] Sanhedrin 97b

PROPHET LIKE MOSES
נביא כמשה

The LORD your God will raise up for you a prophet like me from among you, from your countrymen, you shall listen to him.

Deuteronomy 18:15

SUMMARY: Messiah will be a prophet like Moses and will faithfully speak God's Word. Anyone who does not listen to the Messiah will be held accountable.

This prediction was fulfilled at Messiah's first coming.[513]

This prophecy was seen by many rabbis as referring to Joshua. Rabbi Levi ben Gershon saw Deuteronomy 18:15 as a reference to Messiah.[514]

Related texts include: Numbers 12:6-8; Deuteronomy 34:10-12; Jeremiah 30:21; Micah 4:2.

---

[513] Jn 1:45; 6:14; Acts 3:22,23 etc
[514] According to J. Sibley. See commentary in MHMP, p325, Kindle. Sibley also observes that "...Joshua is never regarded or referred to as a prophet." p327

SIN BEARER
סבל עונותם

After he has suffered, he will see the light of life and be satisfied; by knowledge of him my righteous servant will justify many, and he will bear their iniquities.

Isaiah 53:11

SUMMARY: Messiah will suffer and He will bear the sins of others. He will die but be resurrected.[515] By knowledge of the Messiah many will be made righteous.

This prediction was fulfilled at Messiah's first coming. And even now, many are being justified by belief in Him.[516]

Isaiah 52:13-53:12 was considered messianic by many early rabbinic authorities.

Related texts include: Genesis 22:8; Isaiah 53:4-10,12.

---

[515] The suffering noted in Isa 53:11 is shown to include death in verses 7-10 and 12.
[516] Rom 4:25; 2 Cor 5:21

SERVANT OF THE LORD
עבד יהוה

See, my servant will act wisely; he will be raised and lifted up and highly exalted. Just as there were many who were appalled at him - his appearance was so disfigured beyond that of any human being and his form marred beyond human likeness.

Isaiah 52:13-14

SUMMARY: Messiah will be the LORD's Servant and will succeed in His mission. Though disfigured, humiliated and despised, He will be supremely exalted.

This prediction was fulfilled by Messiah's first coming and His ascension.[517]

Isaiah 52:13 was widely considered messianic.[518]

Related texts include: Psalm 110:1; Isaiah 6:1; 42:1-4; 49:7; 50:4-10; 61:1-11.

---

[517] Matt 27:26,35; Phil 2:9
[518] e.g. LTJM, App9: "Verse 13 is applied in the Targum expressly to the Messiah."

WONDERFUL COUNSELLOR

פלא יועץ

For to us a child is born, to us a son is given, and the government will be on his shoulders. And he will be called Wonderful Counselor, Mighty God, Everlasting Father, Prince of Peace. Of the greatness of his government and peace there will be no end. He will reign on David's throne and over his kingdom, establishing and upholding it with justice and righteousness from that time on and forever.

Isaiah 9:6,7[519]

SUMMARY: Messiah will be a child who will go on to rule over David's kingdom. He will bring peace to Israel and will bear divine titles. His kingdom will never end.

Portions of this prophecy were fulfilled at Messiah's first coming. The establishment of His kingdom and His reign from David's throne awaits future fulfillment.

Some rabbinic sources viewed the passage as messianic.[520]

Related texts include: Isaiah 11:1-12; Jeremiah 23:5; Zechariah 2:10-11.

---

[519] Isa 9:5,6 in the Hebrew text.
[520] LTJM, App9: "Is. ix. 6 is expressly applied to the Messiah in the Targum…"

RIGHTEOUS BRANCH
צמח צדיק

"The days are coming," declares the LORD, "when I will raise up for David a righteous branch, a King who will reign wisely and do what is just and right in the land. In his days Judah will be saved and Israel will live in safety. This is the name by which he will be called: The LORD Our Righteous Saviour.

Jeremiah 23:5-6

SUMMARY: Messiah will be Israel's king, a righteous branch from the line of David. Under His rule the remnant of Israel will be regathered to the Land where they will live in peace and security.

This prediction relates mostly to Messiah's second coming.

Jeremiah 23:5-6 was considered messianic by various ancient rabbis.[521]

Related texts include: Isaiah 4:2; 9:6-7; Psalm 24:7-10; 102:13-17; Zechariah 3:8.

---

[521] *WRSM*, p23,32
LTJM, App9: "On Jer. xxiii. 5, 6, the Targum has it: 'And I will raise up for David the Messiah the Just.' This is one of the passages from which according to Rabbinic views, one of the Names of the Messiah is derived, viz: Jehovah our Righteousness…"

CALLED IN RIGHTEOUSNESS
קרא בצדק

I, the LORD, have called you in righteousness; I will take hold of your hand. I will keep you and will make you to be a covenant for the people and a light for the Gentiles...

Isaiah 42:6

SUMMARY: Messiah, God's servant, will be marked by righteousness. He will embody and fulfill God's covenants with Israel and He will bring light to non-Jews.

This prophecy relates to Messiah's entire career and mission.

Isaiah 42 was considered messianic by a number of rabbinic authorities.[522]

Related texts include: Isaiah 11:5; 49:8; 52:15; 53:11; Jeremiah 23:5.

---

[522] See sources in *WRSM*, p16,17

CHIEF CORNERSTONE
ראש פנה

The stone which the builders rejected has become the chief cornerstone.

Psalms 118:22

SUMMARY: Messiah, though initially rejected as unfit by those in authority in Israel, will be vindicated by the LORD and given the place of preeminence and supreme honour.

Both comings of Messiah are seen in this prophecy: His rejection by Israel and His subsequent acceptance.[523]

Rashi, in his commentary on Micah 5, sees this text as messianic.[524]

Related texts include: Isaiah 8:14; 28:16; 49:7; 53:3-4; Daniel 2:44,45.

---

[523] Psalm 118 is quite frequently referenced or alluded to in the NT: Matt 21:9,42; Luke 20:17-19; Acts 4:1-11; 1 Pet 2:6-8

[524] https://www.chabad.org/library/bible_cdo/aid/16191/showrashi/true

SHILOH
שילה

The sceptre will not depart from Judah nor the ruler's staff from between his feet, until he comes to whom it belongs; the obedience of the nations will be his.

Genesis 49:10

SUMMARY: Messiah will be a descendant of Judah, a King to whom all nations will owe obedience. He will come before Judah loses its tribal identity.

This prophecy relates to both comings of Messiah. The submission of the nations will occur at His second coming. Some translations treat Shiloh as a proper noun but a number of commentators argue that Shiloh should be translated "He to whom it belongs".[525]

Genesis 49:10 was considered messianic by Rashi and others.[526]

Related texts include: Numbers 24:17-20; Isaiah 9:6-7; Ezekiel 21:27; Daniel 7:13,14; 9:24-27.

---

[525] e.g. MIOT, p51

[526] *WRSM*, p17

LTJM, App9: "*Gen. xlix.* 10. This well-known prediction… …is in Yalkut, u. s., applied to the Messiah, with a quotation of Ps. ii. 9…. '…Shiloh' is also applied to the Messiah, with the curious addition, that in the latter days all nations would bring gifts to Him. Alike the Targum Onkelos, Pseudo-Jonathan, and the Jerusalem Targum, as well as Sanh. 98 *b*, the Midrash…"

HIS LAW WILL GO FORTH
תצא תורתו

Many nations will come and say, "Come and let us go up to the mountain of the LORD and to the house of the God of Jacob, that He may teach us about His ways and that we may walk in His paths." For from Zion will go forth the law, even the word of the LORD from Jerusalem.

Micah 4:2

SUMMARY: Messiah will regather and restore Israel, and rule from Jerusalem. He will bring peace to the nations. Many from the nations will go up to Jerusalem, from which His law will go forth to the entire world.

This prophecy will be fulfilled at Messiah's return.

There is evidence that the passage was considered messianic.[527]

Related texts include: Psalm 2:6-10; Isaiah 11:4; Jeremiah 23:5; Zechariah 2:11; 8:3,20-23; 14:9.

---

[527] The following verse (4:3) was seen as messianic. LTJM, App9: "The promise in *Micah iv.* 3 is applied to the times of the Messiah in the Talmud (Shabb. 63 *a*)."

Appendix

ANTISEMITISM

A Brief Survey[528]

Introduction and Definition

"*An antisemite is one who hates Jews more than absolutely necessary*".

I n many cultures antisemitism is *a given*. This is exemplified by the above statement, believed to have originated in Hungary.

The *fact* of antisemitism may be a constant. Its *form*, however, morphs and adapts from age to age and culture to culture. This brief article provides a survey of some of antisemitism's current manifestations and some of the social groups in which antisemitism is most prevalent.

By most accounts, the term *anti-Semitism* was first coined by German journalist Wilhelm Marr in 1879 as a functional equivalent to *Judenhass* - Jew

---

[528] Written in 2021 for the *Holocaust and Antisemitism Foundation, Aotearoa New Zealand*

hatred. While the term is modern, the hatred itself dates back more than 3000 years.

The spelling *antisemitism* is to be preferred to *anti-Semitism* for at least two reasons:

- *Semitism* is not a word;
- to dull the impact of those who engage in fallacious reasoning by insisting that Arabs can not be *anti-Semites* because they too are *Semites*.

Hostility toward or discrimination against Jews as a religious, ethnic, or racial group is the definition provided by Merriam-Webster.

The International Holocaust Remembrance Alliance is an intergovernmental body founded in 1998.[529] IHRA's working definition of antisemitism begins thus:[530]

Antisemitism is a certain perception of Jews, which may be expressed as hatred toward Jews. Rhetorical and physical manifestations of antisemitism are directed toward Jewish or non-Jewish individuals and/

---

[529] Originally named Task Force for International Cooperation on Holocaust Education, Remembrance, and Research.
In 2022 NZ officially took on observer status with IHRA. Observer status does not mean that NZ has, or will necessarily, adopt the IHRA definition of antisemitism.
[530] https://www.holocaustremembrance.com/working-definition-antisemitism

or their property, toward Jewish community institutions and religious facilities.

The non-binding definition is significantly strengthened by an accompanying set of examples considered to form part of the definition. Excerpts of the IHRA definition text, including selected examples of antisemitism, is reproduced below.[531]

Antisemitism has proven to be remarkable in its persistence, pervasion, and versatility. It will reinvent itself as the need arises.

ANTI-ZIONIST ANTISEMITISM

To understand anti-Zionism one must first define Zionism. While historically it is a broad and non-monolithic movement, Zionism can be seen as:

---

[531] Manifestations might include the targeting of the state of Israel, conceived as a Jewish collectivity. However, criticism of Israel similar to that leveled against any other country can not be regarded as antisemitic…
[Amongst the examples cited by IHRA are:]
Denying the Jewish people their right to self-determination, e.g., by claiming that the existence of a State of Israel is a racist endeavor.
Applying double standards by requiring of it a behaviour not expected or demanded of any other democratic nation.
Using the symbols and images associated with classic antisemitism (e.g., claims of Jews killing Jesus or blood libel) to characterize Israel or Israelis.
Drawing comparisons of contemporary Israeli policy to that of the Nazis.
Holding Jews collectively responsible for actions of the state of Israel.

The movement supporting the return of Jews to their ancestral indigenous homeland and their right of national self-determination in the now established State of Israel.

Among modern antisemites of all stripes, the weapon of choice is frequently anti-Zionism. For that reason it is mentioned first in this survey.

As noted, antisemitism is a most creative and resourceful hatred, always able to morph and adapt to a cultural and historical context. For much of the last two millennia antisemitism manifested as religious hatred. In the Nazi period it took on a more racial and "scientific" justification. Now that there is a reborn Jewish state, antisemitism frequently dresses in the garb of human rights,[532] enabling it to freely parade in western societies as anti-Zionism. While hatred of Jews remains somewhat uncouth, hatred of the Jewish state often gets a free pass. It is somehow deemed acceptable to vilify the Jewish state, especially if one first claims to have Jewish friends.

Of course, criticism of the Jewish state is not automatically antisemitic, and definitions such as IHRA's correctly acknowledge this fact. But criti-

[532] The mutation phenomenon was best articulated by recently deceased Lord Rabbi Sacks: https://tinyurl.com/5cdbu29s
Sacks tended to see scapegoating as a primary cause of anti-semitism.

cism of Israel that applies a standard that is applied to no other nation is usually antisemitic. An anti-Zionist's true motivation is usually exposed when asked questions such as:

To which other indigenous group do you deny the right of self-determination in ancestral lands?[533]

To which other people group do you deny the right of appropriate self defence against the aggression of multiple genocidal enemies?

Criticism of Israel need not be antisemitic[534] but her most vocal critics are betrayed by their overt double standards. For example, anti-Zionists will be highly critical of Israel, ostensibly on human

---

[533] Arguably, no people group can lay stronger claim to indigenous status than the Jews. Their connection to the land of Israel is 4000 years old and remarkably well attested by archaeology, literature, religious ritual, and genetics.
https://tinyurl.com/4dy3w5a5
https://tinyurl.com/53m358ze
https://tinyurl.com/ywftxp24

[534] The present writer is critical of certain aspects of Israeli society and policy.

rights grounds, but have little or nothing to say about Israel's neighbours.[535]

Anti-Zionism often denies to one people group (the Jews) what it readily grants to others, and as such is plainly antisemitic. The aforementioned denial of the right of self-determination in one's indigenous homeland, or the right to self defence, are but two examples that expose the antisemitic core of most anti-Zionism.

FAR RIGHT ANTISEMITISM

Today's white supremacy and neo-Nazism stand in continuity with 1930-40s Nazism. Traditional Christian antisemitic ideas and xenophobic nationalism play an important role along with conspiracy theories and Holocaust denial.

In the UK, Europe and USA, far-right antisemites pose a significant threat to Jewish communities. A 2018 attack by a white supremacist on Pittsburgh's Tree of Life Synagogue saw eleven murdered and in the period since the massacre, the city has be-

---

[535] Syria, for example, has barrel bombed and gassed its own citizens while Israel, as the only western style democracy in the Middle East, is the safest place for Christians and provides Arabs greater freedoms than in any Arab state.
According to Randall Price: "Similarly, it has been observed that the death toll in a single day of the Syrian conflict is more than that of all the wars and conflicts between Israel and the Arab world combined!"
Price, *What Should We Think About Israel?: Separating Fact from Fiction in the Middle East Conflict*

come a pilgrimage destination for white suprema-
cists who view the perpetrator as an inspiration.[536]

Riding on a wave of anti-immigration sentiment,
far-right political parties in France, Germany, Aus-
tria and elsewhere, have achieved significant gains
and have contributed to a surge in
antisemitism.[537]

The rise of ethno-nationalism in Eastern and Central Europe has been accompanied by Holocaust
distortion in which local perpetrators and collabo-
rators have been recast as national heroes.[538]Anti-
semitism has risen accordingly.

Laws have been passed effectively exonerating na-
tionals of complicity in the Holocaust and potentially making an accurate telling of Holocaust history a criminal offence.[539]

---

[536] https://forward.com/news/458887/2-years-after-the-synagogue-
shooting-pittsburgh-has-become-a-hub-for-white/

[537] https://www.haaretz.com/world-news/europe/.premium-in-aus-
tria-and-germany-the-nazis-political-heirs-still-want-a-judenfrei-
europe-1.7297946

[538] https://www.ijn.com/on-holocaust-culpability-lithuania-follow-
ing-polands-example/

[539] https://www.israelnationalnews.com/News/News.aspx/274580
https://blogs.timesofisrael.com/lithuanias-misguided-holocaust-
law/

Progressive Leftist Antisemitism

Amidst the identity politics, wokeness, victim-hood olympics, and anti-liberal "liberalism" that mark the progressive left, antisemitism is readily apparent,[540] and too often gets a free pass.[541]

America's academia and broader culture have been greatly influenced by Critical Race Theory, under which, according to Dr James Lindsay, Jews are represented as having "an intolerable privilege they need to check".[542]

Ethnic Studies initiatives have promoted the Boycott Divest Sanction movement and, in the words of one critic, "cleansed Jews from history".[543] The post-colonialist embrace of anti-Zionism similarly results in difficult conditions for Zionist Jews.[544]

Black Lives Matter protests have seen synagogues vandalised and crowds chanting "dirty Jews".[545]

---

[540] https://www.nationalreview.com/2019/05/progressive-anti-semitism-multicultural-left-new-york-times/

[541] https://thefederalist.com/2018/04/06/why-does-the-left-get-a-pass-on-anti-semitism/

[542] https://newdiscourses.com/2020/10/critical-race-theorys-jewish-problem/

[543] https://www.tabletmag.com/sections/news/articles/california-ethnic-studies-curriculum

[544] https://www.sdjewishworld.com/2020/12/17/campus-radicals-equate-zionism-with-white-supremacy/

[545] https://besacenter.org/perspectives-papers/black-lives-matter-antisemitism/
https://www.telegraph.co.uk/women/politics/black-lives-matter-protests-catalyst-anti-semitism/

Certain leaders of the Women's March have been reported as openly antisemitic.[546]

Intersectionality brings together disparate causes and has demonstrated great utility in advancing antisemitism. Hatred for "the Zionist entity" seems to function both as a ticket for admission and a glue that binds, as is evident in the red-green axis.[547] Protests over police brutality have in some cases led to an upsurge in Jew hatred.[548]

The uniqueness of Jewish history, culture and identity, resilience despite centuries of oppression, over achievement[549] and national self-determination, ill-fit a progressive movement fixated on power structures, grievance, anti-nationalism and sameness of outcome.

Among the many long-held ideals targeted by Critical Race Theory is meritocracy. Perhaps because Jews have flourished in societies where they have been granted freedom, they are now assigned to the "white oppressor class", despite the fact that

---

[546] https://nypost.com/2019/09/21/the-womens-march-still-has-an-anti-semitism-problem/

[547] https://www.newsweek.com/worlds-red-green-axis-has-come-our-streets-opinion-1520116

[548] https://www.meforum.org/61385/joffe-on-anti-zionism-and-antisemitism

[549] Typically, at least 20% of Nobel prize winners are Jewish, despite Jews being only approximately 0.2% of the world population.

the majority of Jews are non-white and that Jews are one of history's most oppressed people groups.

ISLAMIC ANTISEMITISM

All societies exhibit antisemitism to some degree, but Jew hatred is disproportionately evident within Islamic communities. In many nations with large Muslim populations, Jews are viewed "very unfavourably" by overwhelming majorities.[550] The Anti-Defamation League reports antisemitic attitudes at 49% in Germany's Muslim community as against 14% amongst Christians.[551]

Islamic antisemitism makes use of a full range of themes and tropes including conspiracies, theological justifications, and racial slurs. Holocaust denial and calls for the destruction of Israel[552] can be heard in mosques worldwide - even in New Zealand.[553]

---

[550] "Anti-Jewish sentiment is endemic in the Muslim world. In Lebanon, all Muslims and 99% of Christians say they have a very unfavorable view of Jews. Similarly, 99% of Jordanians have a very unfavorable view of Jews. Large majorities of Moroccans, Indonesians, Pakistanis and six-in-ten Turks also view Jews unfavorably." https://www.pewresearch.org/global/2005/07/14/islamic-extremism-common-concern-for-muslim-and-western-publics/

[551] https://news.yahoo.com/germany-misleading-classification-anti-semitic-hate-103012722.html

[552] According to Yossi Klein, "The attitude toward the Holocaust in parts of the Muslim world could be summed up, only half-ironically, this way: It never happened, we're glad it did, and we're going to do it again." *Letters to My Palestinian Neighbor* (pp. 189-190).

[553] https://shalom.kiwi/2017/10/shia-leaders-deny-holocaust-call-destruction-israel-new-zealand-mosque/

Understanding and responding to antisemitic incidents is sometimes made more difficult by reluctance of authorities to correctly apportion blame[554] when the incidents are perpetrated by Muslims.

CHRISTIAN ANTISEMITISM

Traditional Christian antisemitism relied heavily on the deicide[555] charge and the blood libel.[556] While these may still be in use, the more "respectable" versions of Christian antisemitism will now use anti-Zionism and alleged human rights concerns.

Undergirding Christian antisemitism is replacement theology.[557] Technically, such theology does not inexorably generate antisemitism. In practice, however, over time it has done so. Efroymson, commenting on the theology of Tertullian observed:

---

[554] https://news.yahoo.com/germany-misleading-classification-anti-semitic-hate-103012722.html
[555] The killing of God.
[556] The ritual murder of Christian children in order to use their blood at Passover.
[557] Or more formally, supersessionism. See Part II

The road from here to Auschwitz is long, and may not be direct, but you can get there from here.[558]

Statements made by Luther in 1543 were among Hitler's justifications for his mass murder of Europe's Jews.[559] Today's most influential Christian antisemites muster theology, professed concern for Palestinians, and anti-Zionism, particularly to undermine evangelical support for Israel.

Prominent examples are the Christian aid agency World Vision[560] and Rev Dr Stephen Sizer, a UK cleric censured[561] by his own Anglican Church for antisemitic activities and endorsed by former UK Labour leader Jeremy Corbyn, also accused of antisemitism.[562]

HUMAN RIGHTS ANTISEMITISM

Human rights organisations currently provide one of the most effective vehicles for antisemitism. The Boycott Divestment Sanctions movement is trans-

---

[558] David P. Efroymson, *Tertullian's Anti-Judaism and Its Role in His Theology* p. 226.

[559] https://www.jewishvirtuallibrary.org/martin-luther-quot-the-jews-and-their-lies-quot

[560] https://www.ngo-monitor.org/ngos/world_vision_international/ https://blogs.timesofisrael.com/world-visions-war-against-the-jewish-state/

[561] https://www.telegraph.co.uk/news/religion/11399986/Vicar-who-blamed-Israel-for-911-attacks-is-banned-from-writing-about-the-Middle-East.html

[562] https://www.smh.com.au/world/europe/jeremy-corbyn-suspended-from-labour-party-after-anti-semitism-report-20201030-p569xl.html

parent in its goal to see the elimination of the Jewish state.563 BDS critiques of Israel frequently compare her conduct to that of Nazi Germany with the "apartheid Israel" charge being equally popular. BDS has been designated "antisemitic" by Germany564 and numerous American states have passed anti-BDS resolutions or laws.565

London-based Amnesty International566 is another human rights body that has been shown to have a strong antisemitic record.567

RACIAL ANTISEMITISM
Most prevalent in Nazi and Muslim circles, racial antisemitism may now be less common in the West having been displaced by other forms of Jew hatred.

References to Jews as "descendants of apes and pigs" remain common in Islamic rhetoric along

563 https://israelinstitute.nz/2018/01/bds-explained-part-i-the-israel-institute-of-new-zealand/

564 https://uk.reuters.com/article/uk-germany-bds-israel/germany-designates-bds-israel-boycott-movement-as-anti-semitic-idUKKC-N1SN1Z3

565 https://www.jewishvirtuallibrary.org/anti-bds-legislation

566https://www.ngo-monitor.org/ngos/amnesty_international/

567 https://www.jewishpress.com/news/israel/boycott/exposed-amnesty-internationals-obsessive-anti-semitic-anti-israel-hatred/2019/12/22/

with such descriptors as "the scum of the human race, the rats of the world".[568]

The Darwinian theories of the time lent justification to the view that the Nazis must "exterminate" the Jews in the interests of Aryan racial purity.

The Khazar theory remains popular. It attempts to sever the link between Jews of the biblical period and the present day by asserting that Ashkenazi Jews are largely descendants of Turkic peoples who converted to Judaism over a thousand years ago.[569]

ECONOMIC ANTISEMITISM

William Shakespeare's *Merchant of Venice* portrays Shylock "the Jew" as avaricious and cruel. Jewish stereotypes of this kind have persisted in literature and discourse to the present day, and readily cross-pollinate other categories of antisemitism presented in this survey.

Jews are held to be excessively wealthy (such wealth achieved by dishonest means and ignoring the many Jews of modest means), greedy and mean (despite Jews being disproportionately rep-

---

[568] https://www.jewishvirtuallibrary.org/muslim-clerics-jews-are-the-descendants-of-apes-pigs-and-other-animals

[569] https://forward.com/opinion/382967/ashkenazi-jews-are-not-khazars-heres-the-proof/
https://elderofziyon.blogspot.com/2014/02/khazar-study-thoroughly-debunked.html

resented amongst philanthropists), and use their wealth to further expand their covert control of media, international politics, world opinion, etc. In this form of antisemitism Jews are accused of driving both capitalism and communism.

Nation of Islam leader Farrakhan provides an example of economic antisemitism:
The Rothschilds financed both sides of all the European wars. They always wanted to get their hands on the Central Bank of America. And they finally did.[570]

Conspiratorial Antisemitism
Many conspiracy theories feature Jews front and centre. Accusations of Jewish control of media, orchestration of financial crises and wars, pedophilia rings, and more, flourish on social media and in far right groups.

Twenty percent of Britons apparently believe Jews concocted the Covid pandemic for financial gain.[571] Throughout the world, many have blamed

[570] Quoted by ADL: https://www.adl.org/resources/backgrounders/jewish-control-of-the-federal-reserve-a-classic-antisemitic-myth
[571] https://www.jpost.com/diaspora/antisemitism/one-in-five-english-people-believe-covid-is-a-jewish-conspiracy-survey-629187

the Jews for 9/11.[572] Jews have even been held responsible for the Holocaust.[573]

The Protocols of the Elders of Zion, 1903, set out a blueprint for Jewish global domination. Despite being demonstrated to be a fabrication in the 1920s it has remained a key document in fuelling antisemitic conspiracy theories to this day. Henry Ford funded and distributed 500,000 copies in the USA and translations of *The Protocols* continue to be important texts for antisemites in Muslim nations.

UNIVERSALIST[574] ANTISEMITISM

The uniqueness and distinction of the Jewish people, their sacred texts and history, longevity and non-assimilation, religious and social separateness, and especially their moral and ethical legacy, have long been a thorn in the side of universalism. A significant theme of 19th century German philosophy was a determination to break the shackles of particularist religion:

...the hegemony of revelation had to be broken. Jews and Judaism were linked to that precise biblical reve-

---

[572] https://www.jewishvirtuallibrary.org/minister-louis-farrakhan-in-his-own-words
[573] https://www.newsweek.com/holocaust-jews-poll-millennials-genz-1531313
[574] Here used in the sense of *universalism* as against *particularism.*

lation that the Enlightenment wanted to free itself of...[575]

Most riling of all is the concept of Jewish chosenness.[576] Despite the Hebrew Scriptures creating at the outset an inextricable link between Jewish chosenness and benefit to *all* nations,[577] chosenness has been construed as elitism, supremacy and arrogance.

The repudiation of uniqueness and particularity by some Jews has done little to alleviate antisemitism. Those Jews who became enamoured with German culture and embraced assimilation in early 20th century Germany, even converting to Christianity and de-Judaizing their names, were no less likely to be found in the cattle trucks destined for Auschwitz.

In the modern period, Israel and the Jews remain distinct. Even those who wholeheartedly embrace

---

[575] *Roots of Theological Anti-Semitism: German Biblical Interpretation and the Jews, from Herder and Semler to Kittel and Bultmann* (Studies in Jewish History and Culture), Anders Gerdmar, p25.

[576] In the view of Nicholson, antisemitism "almost always grows from a resentment of 'chosenness': the idea that the Jewish God appointed one nation, the nation of Israel, to play a special role in history." [Antisemitism] "is a grand anti-myth that turns Jewish chosenness on its head and assigns to the people of Israel responsibility for all the world's ills."
https://tinyurl.com/msvpuwa5

[577] Genesis 12:3

progressive leftist causes can find themselves ostracised if they retain a commitment to Israel.[578]

ANTISEMITISM AT THE UNITED NATIONS

The UN voted in 1947 to partition the British Mandate into two states, one Jewish, one Arab.[579] Israel was reborn 14 May 1948.[580] The UN has since become remarkably hostile to the Jewish state and it serves as a disturbing example of antisemitism's apparent irrationality and increasing momentum.

The UN's severe bias is displayed in its astonishing record of anti-Israel resolutions, in many cases issued under the pretext of human rights concern for the Palestinians.[581] Since 2015 there have been many more condemnatory resolutions against Israel than against all other nations *combined*.[582]

---

[578] https://mosaicmagazine.com/picks/israel-zionism/2019/11/on-the-campus-left-there-is-no-place-for-jews-who-wont-abjure-israel/

[579] Jews accepted partition even though it granted far less than had been hoped for. It excluded most of Judea and Samaria. Arabs rejected the plan and the opportunity for a state. They also rejected statehood offers in 2000 and 2008: https://tinyurl.com/3ktj3zew

[580] Lebanon, Syria, Iraq, Transjordan, and Egypt immediately attacked Israel.

[581] https://unwatch.org/database/

[582] https://unwatch.org/database/
A more recent development:
https://tinyurl.com/4hbx84tw
Late in 2016 NZ co-sponsored the notorious UNSC resolution along with Senegal, Malaysia and Venezuela: https://tinyurl.com/2v5dej95

Jewish presence in Jerusalem[583] seems intolerable to the UN and a recent resolution denied Jewish connection to the city and referenced it only by its Muslim name.[584]

JEWISH ANTISEMITISM

There is often a reflexive rejection of the assertion that Jews can be antisemitic. Examples, however, are not difficult to find.

Karl Marx, one of the most influential individuals of the last two centuries was both Jewish[585] and transparently antisemitic.[586] And Marx is but one in a long lineage of anti-Jewish Jews.[587]

---

[583] In the case of no other nation is the choice of capital city considered controversial by the world community. Many nations have been outspoken in their opposition to Jerusalem as Israel's capital and only USA, Guatemala, Honduras and Kosovo have embassies there: https://tinyurl.com/27v7xfx7

[584] https://www.jpost.com/opinion/article-690000

[585] Critics may claim that Marx converted to Christianity as a child. His father "converted" Karl in an attempt to avoid anti-Jewish legislation. But Marx himself was an atheist and was, and is, regarded a Jew.

[586] According to Joseph Telushkin: 'Less known is that Hitler claimed Marx as a mentor on the Jewish issue: "It is quite enough that the scientific knowledge of the danger of Judaism is gradually deepened and that every individual on the basis of this knowledge begins to eliminate that Jew within himself, and I am very much afraid that this beautiful thought originates from none other than a Jew."' https://www.tabletmag.com/sections/news/articles/black-lives-matter-and-self-hating-jews

[587] https://www.jpost.com/opinion/columnists/wistrich-on-the-left-the-jews-and-israel

"Non-Jewish Jews"[588] or "self-hating Jews"[589] serve an important role for non-Jewish antisemites. They often function as "human shields"[590] for "Jew bashers on the left". It is assumed for example that the hatred espoused for the Jewish state is somehow validated by the presence of Jews in the ranks of haters.

In the present day there are many Jewish individuals and groups who support the antisemitic BDS movement.[591]

Not all Gentiles are antisemites and not all antisemites are Gentiles.

CONCLUSION

It is hoped that the foregoing brief survey has successfully demonstrated the persistence, pervasiveness and peculiarity of antisemitism. *The longest hatred* shows no sign of abating.

---

[588] A term attributed to Jewish historian Isaac Deutscher, according to Dennis Prager:
https://dennisprager.com/column/george-soros-and-the-problem-of-the-radical-non-jewish-jew/

[589] e.g. https://www.tabletmag.com/sections/news/articles/black-lives-matter-and-self-hating-jews
https://www.ynetnews.com/articles/0,7340,L-5065232,00.html
https://www.jpost.com/opinion/article-745296

[590] https://www.jewishpress.com/indepth/opinions/when-the-jew-bashers-are-jews/2021/08/16/

[591] https://www.jpost.com/israel-news/39-jewish-left-wing-groups-pen-letter-supporting-bds-562843

Appendix

The Abstract Palestinian

And The Selective Cry For Justice

C ontemporary forms of replacement theology are frequently accompanied by cries for justice in the face of alleged Israeli outrages against the Palestinians. However, upon examination such cries are often found to be based on highly selective and misleading readings of history and a one-sided narrative, and thus ring somewhat hollow.[592]

---

[592] Two NZ examples: 1. *No Peace Without Justice*, Coleman, Reality Magazine June-July 2002, p13-18
2. Tollestrup in *Israel: 5 Views* misrepresents Israelis, ignores context and goes so far as to claim as "indisputable… …the formation of the state of Israel and Zionist movement… …has been calamitous" for the Palestinians (p28). Little if anything is said about Palestinian intransigence, rejectionism, corruption, incitement to genocidal hatred, and that terrorists are granted hero status. Tollestrup claims as myth "Palestinian resistance is terrorist in character," contrary to data available from Palestinian sources at the time. See: https://www.evangelicalzionism.com/tear-fund-nz-2012
Little has changed. As of March 2023, according to Palestinian sources: *…more than 70% declare support for the latest Huwara shooting attack against settlers…* https://pcpsr.org/en/node/938

The actions of all nations are subject to scrutiny and Israel is no exception. When Israel behaves badly it should be criticised.[593] Valid criticism, however, gives due consideration to context, and does not apply double standards, ignore highly relevant factors, distort history or turn a blind eye to the genocidal intentions of Israel's enemies.

It is not the burden of this book to defend Israeli actions. However, the phenomenon of double standards in the supersessionist anti-Zionist narrative should be noted.

Israel's Christian critics may claim to be primarily concerned for the wellbeing of ordinary Palestinians. However, their near silence regarding the suffering of Palestinian Christians in Palestinian controlled areas brings this into question.[594]

Indigenous rights have become a favoured cause among leftist social justice activists worldwide. But seldom, if ever, do we hear Israel's opponents acknowledge Israel's Jews to be an indigenous

---

[593] Diaspora Jews, Israeli citizens and Israel's judiciary are amongst Israel's harshest critics. The present writer too is critical of aspects of Israeli society and government policy.

[594] Christian Palestinian communities have diminished significantly in Palestinian controlled areas.
https://besacenter.org/persecution-christians-palestinian-authority/
https://www.jewishvirtuallibrary.org/christians-in-the-palestinian-authority

people seeking self-determination in ancestral lands.[595] Likewise, Israel's evangelical critics seem loath to even acknowledge Jewish indigeneity, much less to advocate for such rights.

Seldom, too, do Israel's Christian critics speak of Israel's precarious security situation, the deep corruption of Palestinian leadership, rejectionism, the glorification of terror, and the incitement to hatred even among the youngest Palestinian children in Gaza and the disputed territories.[596]

Israeli citizens (Arab and Jew alike) must contend with Palestinian suicide attacks and rocket fire on civilian areas. This is seldom framed as an injustice against which Christians are urged to rail.[597] When commenting on the case of Arab displacement as a result of Israel's defensive War of Independence, which of the replacement theologians will include within their critique any mention of

---

[595] https://tinyurl.com/4janbz8j
https://www.indigenouscoalition.org/articles-blog/dear-kanoa-not-colonialism

[596] Incitement to hate and violence is a feature of UNRWA funded Palestinian schools. 2023 report: https://unwatch.org/wp-content/uploads/2023/03/2023-Report-UNRWA.pdf

[597] The indiscriminate nature of Palestinian terror means that Arab Israeli citizens suffer from Palestinian terror too.
https://www.indigenouscoalition.org/articles-blog/is-terror-ever-justified
The fact that Arab citizens of Israel enjoy greater freedoms, opportunities and protections than any of their kin in neighbouring Arab nations is seldom mentioned by anti-Zionists. Ignoring such matters does serve to lubricate the activists' narrative, but it brings motivation into question.

the estimated 700,000-1,000,000 Jews expelled from neighbouring lands?[598]

If it is truly justice that motivates Israel's Christian critics, then an explanation for the one-sided narrative and the neglect of suffering Palestinians in areas *not* controlled by Israel is long overdue.

THE ABSTRACT PALESTINIAN

It seems the Palestinians have their greatest utility as assets in the anti-Zionist narrative. The tragic Arab on Arab human rights violations in neighbouring nations have nothing to contribute to such a narrative, so these usually go unmentioned by Israel's supersessionist opponents. Palestinian victims of atrocities committed in nearby lands attract little attention simply because Israel can

---

[598] https://jcpa.org/article/the-expulsion-of-the-jews-from-muslim-countries-1920-1970-a-history-of-ongoing-cruelty-and-discrimination/

Jewish refugees from the surrounding nations were absorbed into Israel or emigrated elsewhere. (Arab refugees were mostly not absorbed into the surrounding Arab nations, thus the current refugee camps.) None of the Jews expelled were compensated for the vast wealth left behind in nations in which they had resided, in most cases, for many centuries.

Arabs in the area of conflict in 1948: 1. left as a result of orders from Arab high command; 2. chose to stay, with many subsequently becoming full citizens of Israel; 3. were expelled or displaced from certain areas for militarily strategic reasons in a defensive war. There was terrible suffering on both sides, as with most wars.

not be blamed for their plight.[599] Thus, it seems that Palestinians are reduced to an abstraction. Their suffering is deemed noteworthy only when it serves an overriding purpose, that being the demonisation of Israel.

Palestinians are too easily stripped of their agency and dignity. Their true value is as actors in a social justice scenario that facilitates accusations against the Jewish state.

Meanwhile, unsurprisingly, the important contributions of the many moderate Palestinians and loyal Arab Israelis are routinely ignored by the replacement theologians so critical of Israel.[600]

---

[599] 'The world, including the United Nations, Europe and other international human rights and "pro-Palestinian" organizations, have not moved to help the Palestinians of Syria in the past nine years…
…Because these Palestinians' problems can not be blamed on Israel.'
Khaled Abu Toameh
https://www.gatestoneinstitute.org/15379/palestinians-syria-death-misery
[600] e.g. Palestinian lawyer filmed in Ramallah:
https://israelinstitute.nz/2018/08/straight-talk-from-the-heart-of-ramallah/
https://israelinstitute.nz/2018/09/straight-talk-from-ramallah-part-2/
Arab Israeli Yoseph Haddad served in the Israel Defence Force as a commander over Jewish soldiers. An interview filmed in Auckland 2023:
https://www.indigenouscoalition.org/articles-blog/stolen-palestinian-land

Recommended Reading

The Coming Kingdom:
What Is the Kingdom and How Is Kingdom Now
Theology Changing the Focus of the Church?
Andy Woods

The Words of the Covenant - A Biblical Theology:
Volume 1 - Old Testament Expectation
Paul Henebury

Our Hands Are Stained with Blood:
The Tragic Story of the Church and the Jewish People
Michael Brown

The God of Israel And Christian Theology
R Kendal Soulen

Future Israel:
Why Christian Anti-Judaism Must Be Challenged
Barry Horner

Eternal Israel: Biblical, Theological, and Historical
Studies That Uphold the Eternal, Distinctive Destiny
of Israel
Barry Horner

Israelology: The Missing Link In Systematic Theology
Arnold Fruchtenbaum

The Moody Handbook of Messianic Prophecy:
Studies and Expositions of the Messiah in the Old Testament
Michael Rydelnik and Edwin Blum (editors)

Why the Jews?: The Reason for Antisemitism
Denis Prager and Joseph Telushkin

What Should We Think About Israel?:
Separating Fact from Fiction in the Middle East
Conflict
Randall Price (editor)

Jerusalem in Prophecy: God's Stage for the Final Drama
Randall Price

They Conspire Against Your People:
The European Churches and the Holocaust
Colin Barnes

The Time is Now! Seven Steps Christians Should
Take To Help All Jewish People
Olivier Melnick

The Case for Zionism:
Why Christians Should Support Israel
Thomas Ice

He Will Reign Forever:
A Biblical Theology of the Kingdom of God
Michael Vlach

The Old in the New: Understanding How the New Testament Authors Quoted the Old Testament
Michael Vlach

Why the Jewish People?:
Understanding Replacement Theology & Anti-semitism
Thomas Fretwell

Why Israel?:
Understanding God's Plan for Israel & the Nations
Thomas Fretwell

Reading Moses, Seeing Jesus:
How the Torah (Law) Fulfills its Goal in Yeshua (Jesus)
Seth Postell, Eitan Bar, Erez Soref

The Messiah in the Old Testament
Walter Kaiser, Jnr

The Jews, Modern Israel and the New Supersessionism
Calvin L Smith (editor)

Recommendation does not necessarily imply agreement with all views held by the respective writers.

Israel in the Biblical Worldview: An Introduction

is available in paperback,
hardcover or Kindle versions
www.amazon.com/dp/0473674009/

Visit the author's website

Sign up for the mailing list